Time for STILL MORE TEA

Bogey says -

WAKE UP

Time for STILL MORE TEA

Wake Up
AMERICA

Ron Berger 2

Time for STILL MORE TEA

America's True Enemies

Ron Berger

Published by:

berger publishing

Rancho Belago, CA 92555
Email - mail@ronberger.com
Web Page - www.ronberger.com

berger publishing

Printed in the USA
ISBN 13 - 978-0-9799257-4-0
ISBN 10 - 0-9799257-4-6
Volume III
First printing
Library of Congress Control Number: 2010921741

Time for STILL MORE TEA

Ron's other books -

The House That Ron Built
(1-4137-8605-7) (978-1-4137-8605-7)
PublishAmerica, LLC

Are You Being Served Yet?
(1-4241-2485-9) (978-14241-2485-5)
PublishAmerica, LLC

P-NUT, The Love of a Dog
(1-59824-303-9) (978-1-59824-303-1)
E-Book Time, LLC

"Normal" MAYDAY
(0-9799257-0-3) (978-0-9799257-0-2)
berger publishing

Time for TEA
(0-9799257-1-1) (978-0-9799257-1-9)
berger publishing

Growing Old is a FULL-TIME JOB
(0-9799257-2-X) (978-0-9799257-2-6)
berger publishing

Time for MORE TEA
(0-9799257-3-8) (978-0-9799257-3-3)
berger publishing

Author's Note:

E-mail messages and article clips used in this book are started with (**) and ended with (****) with credit given if the author and/or source is known.

I beseech everyone, who reads this book, to get involved and to lend their voice in turning this country around. I am not a member of the "radical right" or the "right wing conspiracy" but after reading this you will find that the "radical left" and the "left wing conspiracy" is growing fast. I could write much more, but I don't want you to get bored. I love this country and only want to see it survive.

Join the TEA PARTY while it is still possible.

Contents

About the author   8

Introduction   12

Islam   21

Mexico   112

US Government   179

ABOUT THE AUTHOR

Coming from a small town in Wisconsin, I was never exposed to much in the political realm. My dad was a Democrat, mainly be- cause he was a union worker for the Electric Company, and he only looked for his benefits. My mother was a Republican (I think). Only one election did I get involved enough to actually offer my voting advise. It was 1948 when I heard Harry Truman talk and it made much more sense to me than Thomas Dewey that I advised my mother to vote for Truman. I don't know if she ever did, but Mr Truman was the last Democrat that made sense to me.

The election of 1952 was a no-brainer as far as I was con- cerned. I really felt sorry for Adlai Stevenson - and then for

him to campaign against General
Eisenhower twice in four years
was too much. Even the Democratic party tried to get Ike to
run on their ticket in 1951. He
was my Commander-in-Chief while I
was in the USAF and I was proud
of that fact.

My political life started to
take shape when I was hired by a
builder in California. That family was 100% Republican and you
had better be also if you wanted
to work for them. I didn't have
to make any adjustment in my
thinking and was on board with
them from the first day. Nixon
was our man and Kennedy was not.
The next election in 1964 was
Goldwater and not Johnson. We
all know how those elections
turned out.

During most Local, State and
Federal elections I would automatically vote Republican. That
doesn't mean that I thought they
were better, but rather it was

just easier. During the election of 1992 I broke that pattern and voted for Ross Perot. After he fell flat on his butt, I stopped voting altogether. I really couldn't tell the good from the bad. Oh, I had feelings, but figured that my vote didn't count anyway so why go through the hassle?

The last election between Obama and McCain really got me worked up. Not only did I feel this country now was going down the wrong path, but I felt an urgency about doing something about it. That's what most people felt, but didn't know what they should do about it. After about a year of receiving Obama bashing emails I realized that there has to be some truth to it. Then came the "Tea Party Brigades". I have never seen the general public so worked up and so wanting to turn this country around and take the

control back from the Obama administration.

Now that a year plus has
gone by with B. O. (Barack Obama)
in charge, the meaning of
"change" has really sunk in. He
claimed that the USA was the best
country in the world and he
wanted to "change" it from the
last administration. We now know
that his change means socialism.

Lord, save us from those
that think they know more than
our founding fathers on how to
run this country. This is the
time for a complete change in
Washington, DC.

This is TEA TIME!

INTRODUCTION

During the writing of my previous two TEA books I have become incensed by the actions of "our" government. We are increasingly moving to the Socialistic side and it is not in keeping with our Constitution. More and more evidence is coming my way that just begs me to speak out.

My "Time for TEA" and "Time for MORE TEA" books have just touched on the problems we are facing. We really have three enemies that are already here and are actively moving against us.

Until now, I'm sure most of you believe that we are safe and have nothing to fear. Let me warn you that is not the case and our ability to fight back is being severely hampered and actually propagated by the liberal faction of our government.

The President and Congress have steered our movement in the direction of bankruptcy and Islam. BO has even said that if push comes to shove, he will stand with Islam.

Our children and their children are now saddled with the largest deficit in history. You will be punished if you don't sign up for ObamaCare and you wont be able to sell your house until you have a permit, issued by the government to make sure you are in compliance with all the laws.

That is just two of the problems that face us and are illegal, but have been signed into law by BO. Fixing the immigration problem will be fixed simply by making all the illegals, citizens. Still, being illegals, they have more benefits than citizens.

Our three "true enemies" are the Islamic terrorists, the Mexicans and our own government. You know about the terrorists and you probably still feel that only the "odd ball" terrorist does something in the USA. The people doing things like "the shoe bomber", "the underwear bomber" and the "times square bomber" are "home grown" and there are many more where they came from. There are Islamic cells that are actively recruiting members to do damage to our country.

France, England and Germany are already facing these problems and are frozen on what to do. Europe is already being overwhelmed and will be lost to our cause in the very near future.

Mexico is a silent enemy. They actually support sending illegals to our country so they don't have to deal with them. They also castigate us for sealing our borders to these illegals. Arizona has come under great criticism for the laws they recently passed, both by Mexico and BO.

The Mexican cities closest to the border are complaining that they can't handle all their citizens that are coming back. Isn't that a shame?

Our third enemy is our own government including the President and those liberals in Congress. BO is the worst occupier of the White House since Carter and the liberal leaders in the Senate and the House just follow him around like a puppy, bowing to every whim he murmurs. We have the largest bunch of spineless traitors that ever gathered in one place.

Ron

I'm sorry folks, but this is the turkey that was elected President

Ron Berger 15

Time for STILL MORE TEA

Thank you for reading this book. I know some won't like it, but then again, the truth hurts.

Please join me in the "Tea Party" that is going on as we speak. Nothing is more important than taking back the country that our founding fathers built and restoring our standing in the world.

www.teapartynation.com
www.teapartypatriots.com

Your participation is needed.

Thanks, Ron

May God Bless You All

Dear Ron,
"Thank you so much for sending me a copy of your book. You're a true patriot! Please continue to let your voice be heard. Todd and I were happy to receive your message and we appreciate your thoughtfulness for taking the time to write. . . "

Sarah Palin

Sarah Palin might look like a powder puff and all feminine but you can rest assured that she can be tough as nails. She proved it in Alaska and she would do it in the White House. We need this kind of leadership now. She would give the other countries the feeling that she is a pushover and when they tried to turn the tables on us she would kick their butts just like she did with big oil in Alaska.

One thing is for sure - she would not bow to all those "foreign powers" and ask for forgiveness. We have way to many of our service people buried on their lands for us to ask for forgiveness. First of all - who the hell do they think they are? Who was always there to help them out. Who is the lead country fighting the battle against the terrorists so that all may benefit?

ISLAM

NUMBER ONE TO START THE APOCALYPSE

I hope and pray that a new war doesn't start on the BO watch. I would believe that we wouldn't take up the fight and we would try and negotiate our way out. BO would never call for hostilities against his Muslims. His administration can not even bear to call the "times square bomber" a terrorist. The entire administration is so attuned to BO and his radical thinking that they wouldn't dare to contradict what he wants. His troops are all law breaking, mealy mouth, lying, tax avoiding, spineless nincompoops that should never have been brought into the government.

This is an example of a person who can't call a spade a spade:

**

By: Stephen Dinan
Despite crediting the Pakistani Taliban with fostering the recent failed car bombing in Times Square, Attorney General Eric H. Holder Jr. was reluctant Thursday to say

radical Islam was part of the cause of that and other recent attacks.

Mr. Holder, testifying to the House Judiciary Committee, repeatedly balked at a half-dozen questions from Rep. Lamar Smith, the ranking Republican on the committee, about whether "radical Islam" was behind the attempted car bombing, last year's so-called "underpants bomber" or the killings at Fort Hood in Texas.

"There are a variety of reasons why people do these things. Some of them are potentially religious," Mr. Holder told the committee Thursday, though he would not go further than saying people who hold radical views may have "had an ability to have an impact" on Faisal Shahzad, the man the Justice Department says tried to detonate a car bomb in Times Square.

****

Islam is all around us. Here is a breakdown as to how far they have penetrated so far:

**

A BETTER UNDERSTANDING OF THE LONG TERM MUSLIM AGENDA.

Adapted from   Dr. Peter Hammond's book: Slavery, Terrorism and Islam: The Historical Roots and Contemporary Threat.

Islam is not a religion, nor is it a cult. In its fullest form, it is a complete, total, 100% system of life.

Islam has   religious, legal, political, eco - nomic, social, and military components. The religious component is a beard for all of the other components.

Islamization begins when there are suffi-
cient Muslims in a country to agitate for
their religious privileges.

When politically correct, tolerant, and culturally diverse societies agree to Muslim
demands for their religious privileges, some
of the other components tend to creep in
as well.

Here's how it works:

As long as the Muslim population remains
around or under 2% in any given country,
they will be for the most part be regarded
as a peace-loving minority, and not as a
threat to other citizens. This is the case in:

United States -- Muslim 0.6%
Australia -- Muslim 1.5%
Canada -- Muslim 1.9%
China -- Muslim 1.8%

Italy -- Muslim 1.5%
Norway -- Muslim 1.8%

At 2% to 5%, they begin to proselytize from other ethnic minorities and disaffected groups, often with major recruiting from the jails and among street gangs. This is happening in:

Denmark -- Muslim 2%
Germany -- Muslim 3.7%
United Kingdom -- Muslim 2.7%
Spain -- Muslim 4%
Thailand -- Muslim 4.6%

From 5% on, they exercise an inordinate influence in proportion to their percentage of the population. For example, they will push for the introduction of halal (clean by Islamic standards) food, thereby securing food preparation jobs for Muslims. They will increase pressure on supermarket

chains to feature halal on their shelves --
along with threats for failure to comply.
This is occurring in:

France -- Muslim 8%
Philippines -- 5%
Sweden -- Muslim 5%
Switzerland -- Muslim 4.3%
The Netherlands -- Muslim 5.5%
Trinidad & Tobago -- Muslim 5.8%

At this point, they will work to get the ruling government to allow them to rule
themselves (within their ghettos) under
Sharia, the Islamic Law. The ultimate goal
of Islamists is to establish Sharia law over
the entire world.

When Muslims approach 10% of the
population, they tend to increase lawless -
ness as a means of complaint about their
conditions. In Paris, we are already seeing

car-burnings.   Any non-Muslim action offends Islam and results   in uprisings and
threats, such as in Amsterdam, with opposition to   Mohammed cartoons and films
about Islam.   Such tensions are seen daily,
particularly in Muslim sections in:

Guyana -- Muslim 10%
India -- Muslim 13.4%
Israel -- Muslim 16%
Kenya -- Muslim 10%
Russia -- Muslim 15%

After   reaching 20%, nations can expect
hair-trigger rioting, jihad militia formations,
sporadic killings, and the burnings of Christian churches and   Jewish synagogues,
such as in:

Ethiopia -- Muslim 32.8%

At 40%, nations experience widespread massacres, chronic terror attacks, and on-going militia warfare, such as in:

Bosnia -- Muslim 40%
Chad -- Muslim 53.1%
Lebanon -- Muslim 59.7%

From 60%, nations experience unfettered persecution of non-believers of all other re-ligions   (including non-conforming Mus -lims), sporadic ethnic cleansing (genocide), use of Sharia Law as a weapon, and Jizya, the tax placed on infidels, such as in:

Albania -- Muslim 70%
Malaysia -- Muslim 60.4%
Qatar -- Muslim 77..5%
Sudan -- Muslim 70%

After 80%, expect daily intimidation and violent jihad, some State-run ethnic cleans-

ing, and even some genocide, as these nations drive out the   infidels, and move toward 100% Muslim, such as has been ex-
perienced and in   some ways is on-going
in:

Bangladesh -- Muslim 83%
Egypt -- Muslim 90%
Gaza -- Muslim 98.7%
Indonesia -- Muslim 86.1%
Iran -- Muslim 98%
Iraq -- Muslim 97%
Jordan -- Muslim 92%
Morocco -- Muslim 98.7%
Pakistan -- Muslim 97%
Palestine -- Muslim 99%
Syria -- Muslim 90%
Tajikistan -- Muslim 90%
Turkey -- Muslim 99.8%
United Arab Emirates -- Muslim 96%

100% will usher in the peace of 'Dar-es-Salaam' -- the Islamic House of Peace. Here there's supposed to be peace, because everybody is a Muslim, the Madrasses are the only schools, and the Koran is the only word, such as in:

Afghanistan -- Muslim 100%
Saudi Arabia -- Muslim 100%
Somalia -- Muslim 100%
Yemen -- Muslim 100%

Unfortunately, peace is never achieved, as in these 100% states the most radical Muslims intimidate and spew hatred, and satisfy their blood lust by killing less radical Muslims, for a variety of reasons.

'Before I was nine I had learned the basic canon of Arab life. It was me against my brother; me and my brother against our father; my family against my cousins and the clan; the clan against the tribe; the tribe against the world, and all of us against the infidel. -- Leon Uris, 'The Haj'

It is important to understand that in some countries, with well under 100% Muslim populations, such as France, the minority Muslim populations live in ghettos, within which they are 100% Muslim, and within which they live by Sharia Law. The national police do not even enter these ghettos.   There are no national courts, nor schools, nor non-Muslim religious facilities.
In such situations, Muslims do not integrate into the community at large. The children attend madrasses.   They learn only the Koran. To even associate with an infidel is a   crime punishable with death.
Therefore, in some areas of certain nations, Muslim Imams and extremists exercise more power than the national average would indicate.

Today's 1.5 billion Muslims make up 22% of the world's population. But their birth rates dwarf the birth rates of Christians, Hindus, Buddhists, Jews, and all other believers. Muslims will exceed 50% of the world's population by the end of this century.

Adapted from Dr. Peter Hammond's book: Slavery, Terrorism and Islam: The Historical Roots and Contemporary Threat.

Well, boys and girls, today we are letting the fox guard the henhouse. The wolves will be herding the sheep!

Obama appoints two devout Muslims to Homeland Security posts. Doesn't this make you feel safer already?

Obama and Janet Napolitano appoint Arif Alikhan, a devout Muslim, as Assistant Secretary for Policy Development.

DHS Secretary Janet Napolitano swore in Kareem Shora, a devout Muslim who was born in Damascus, Syria, as ADC National Executive Director as a member of the Homeland Security Advisory Council (HSAC).

NOTE: Has anyone ever heard a new government official being identified as a devout Catholic, a devout Jew or a devout Protestant...? Just wondering.

Devout Muslims being appointed to critical Homeland Security positions? Doesn't this make you feel safer already??
Was it not "Devout Muslim men" who flew planes into U.S. buildings 8 years ago?

Was it not a Devout Muslim who killed 13 at Fort Hood?

****

Europe already has the problem of how to deal with Islam. It is not a religion, per se, but a way of life that is not peaceful. They are taught young to kill the infidels. Just read the Quran and find out.

**

'In a generation or two, the   US will ask itself: who lost Europe ?'

Here is   the speech of Geert Wilders, Chairman, Party for Freedom, the Netherlands , at the Four Seasons, New York , introducing an Alliance of Patriots and announcing the Facing Jihad Conference in

Jerusalem .

Dear friends,

Thank you very much for inviting me.

I come to   America with a mission. All is
not well in the old   world.   There is a tremendous danger   looming, and it is very
difficult to be   optimistic.   We might be in
the final   stages of the Islamization of
Europe. This not only is a clear and pre-
sent danger to the   future of Europe itself,
it is a threat to   America and the sheer
survival of the West.   The   United States
as the last bastion of Western   civilization,
facing an Islamic Europe.

First I will describe the   situation on the
ground in Europe .   Then, I will say a few
things about Islam. To close I will tell you
about a meeting in   Jerusalem .

The Europe you know is changing.

You have probably seen the landmarks. But in all of these cities, sometimes a few blocks away from your tourist destination, there is another world. It is the world of the parallel society created by Muslim mass-migration.

All throughout Europe a new reality is rising: entire Muslim neighborhoods where very few indigenous people reside or are even seen. And if they are, they might regret it. This goes for the police as well. It's the world of head scarves, where women walk around in figureless tents, with baby strollers and a group of children. Their husbands, or slaveholders if you prefer, walk three steps ahead. With mosques on many street corners. The shops have signs you and I cannot read.

You will be hard-pressed to find any economic activity.. These are Muslim ghettos controlled by religious fanatics. These are Muslim neighborhoods, and they are mushrooming in every city across Europe. These are the building-blocks for territorial control of increasingly larger portions of Europe, street by street, neighborhood by neighborhood, city by city.

There are now thousands of mosques throughout Europe. With larger congregations than there are in churches. And in every European city there are plans to build super-mosques that will dwarf every church in the region. Clearly, the signal is: we rule.

Many European cities are already one-quarter Muslim: just take Amsterdam, Marseille and Malmo in Sweden. In many cities the majority of the under-18

population is Muslim.   Paris is now sur-
rounded by a ring of Muslim   neighborhoods.   Mohammed is the most popular
name among boys in many cities.

In some elementary schools in   Amsterdam the   farm can no longer be mentioned, because that   would also mean
mentioning the pig, and that   would be an
insult to Muslims.

Many state   schools in Belgium and
Denmark only serve halal food to all pupils.
In   once-tolerant Amsterdam gays   are
beaten up almost exclusively by Muslims.
Non-Muslim women routinely hear 'whore,
whore'. Satellite dishes are not pointed to
local TV stations, but to stations in the
country of origin.

In   France school teachers are advised to
avoid authors deemed   offensive to Mus-

lims, including Voltaire and Diderot; the same is increasingly true of Darwin . The history of the Holocaust can no longer be taught because of Muslim sensitivity.

In England sharia courts are now officially part of the British legal system. Many neighborhoods in France are no-go areas for women without head scarves. Last week a man almost died after being beaten up by Muslims in Brussels , because he was drinking during the Ramadan.

Jews are fleeing France in record numbers, on the run for the worst wave of anti-Semitism since World War II. French is now commonly spoken on the streets of Tel Aviv and Netanya , Israel . I could go on forever with stories like this. Stories about Islamization.

A total of fifty-four million Muslims now live in Europe. San Diego University recently calculated that a staggering 25 percent of the population in Europe will be Muslim just 12 years from now. Bern-hard Lewis has predicted a Muslim major-ity by the end of this century.

Now these are just numbers. And the numbers would not be threatening if the Muslim-immigrants had a strong desire to assimilate. But there are few signs of that. The Pew Research Center re-ported that half of French Muslims see their loyalty to Islam as greater than their loy-alty to France . One-third of French Muslims do not object to suicide attacks.. The British Centre for Social Cohesion re-ported that one-third of British Muslim stu-dents are in favor of a worldwide caliph-ate. Muslims demand what they call 're-spect'. And this is how we give them respect. We have Muslim official state holi-days.

The Christian-Democratic attorney general is willing to accept sharia in the Nether-lands if there is a Muslim majority. We have cabinet members with passports from Morocco and Turkey .

Muslim demands are supported by unlaw-ful behavior, ranging from petty crimes and random violence, for example against am-bulance workers and bus drivers, to small-scale riots. Paris has seen its uprising in the low-income suburbs, the banlieus. I call the perpetrators 'settlers'. Because that is what they are.. They do not come to integrate into our societies; they come to integrate our society into their Dar-al-Islam. Therefore, they are settlers.

Much of this street violence I mentioned is

directed   exclusively against non-Muslims, forcing many   native people to leave their neighborhoods,   their cities, their countries.. Moreover,   Muslims are now a swing vote not to be ignored.

The second thing you need to know is the importance of Mohammed the   prophet. His behavior is an example to all   Muslims and cannot be criticized.   Now, if Mo - hammed had been a man of peace, let us say   like Ghandi and Mother Theresa wrapped in one,   there would be no prob- lem.   But Mohammed   was a warlord, a mass murderer, a pedophile, and   had sev- eral marriages - at the same time.   Islamic tradition tells us how he fought in   battles, how he had his enemies murdered and even had prisoners of war executed.   Mo- hammed himself slaughtered the Jewish tribe of Banu Qurayza. If it is good for Is- lam, it   is good.   If it is bad for Islam, it is bad.

Let no one fool you about Islam being a
religion. Sure, it has a god, and a here-
after, and 72 virgins. But in its essence
Islam is a political ideology.. It is a system
that lays down detailed rules for society
and the life of every person. Islam wants
to dictate every aspect of life. Islam
means 'submission' . Islam is not com-
patible with freedom and democracy, because what it strives for is sharia. If you
want to compare Islam to anything, com-
pare it to communism or national-
socialism, these are all totalitarian ideolo-
gies.

Now you know why Winston Churchill
called Islam 'the most retrograde force in
the world', and why he compared Mein
Kampf to the Quran. The public has
wholeheartedly accepted the Palestinian

narrative, and sees Israel as the aggressor. I have lived in this country and visited it dozens of times. I support Israel . First, because it is the Jewish homeland after two thousand years of exile up to and including Auschwitz, second because it is a democracy, and third because Israel is our first line of defense.

This tiny country is situated on the fault line of jihad, frustrating Islam's territorial advance. Israel is facing the front lines of jihad, like Kashmir, Kosovo, the Philippines , Southern Thailand, Darfur in Sudan, Lebanon , and Aceh in Indonesia. Israel is simply in the way. The same way West-Berlin was during the Cold War.

The war against Israel is not a war against Israel. It is a war against the West. It is jihad. Israel is simply receiving the blows that are meant for all of us. If there

would have been no   Israel , Islamic im-
perialism would have found other venues to
release its energy and its desire for con-
quest. Thanks to Israeli parents who send
their children to the army and lay awake at
night, parents in Europe and America can
sleep well and dream, unaware of the dan-
gers looming.

Many in Europe argue in favor of abandoning Israel in order to address the grievances of our Muslim minorities. But if Israel were, God   forbid, to go down, it
would not bring any solace to the West It
would not mean our Muslim minorities
would all of a sudden change their behavior, and accept our values. On the con-
trary, the end of Israel would give enor-
mous encouragement to the forces of Islam. They would, and rightly so, see the
demise of Israel as proof that the West is
weak, and doomed. The end of Israel

would not mean the end of our problems with Islam, but only the beginning. It would mean the start of the final battle for world domination. If they can get Israel, they can get everything. So-called journalists volunteer to label any and all critics of Islamization as a 'right-wing extremists' or 'racists'. In my country, the Netherlands , 60 percent of the population now sees the mass immigration of Muslims as the number one policy mistake since World War II. And another 60 percent sees Islam as the biggest threat. Yet there is a danger greater danger than terrorist attacks, the scenario of America as the last man standing. The lights may go out in Europe faster than you can imagine. An Islamic Europe means a Europe without freedom and democracy, an economic wasteland, an intellectual nightmare, and a loss of military might for America - as its allies will turn into enemies, enemies with atomic bombs.   With an Islamic Europe,   it would be up to America alone to preserve the heritage of Rome , Athens and Jerusa-lem .

Dear friends, liberty is the most precious of gifts. My generation never had to fight for this freedom, it was offered to us on a silver platter, by people who fought for it with their lives. All throughout   Europe , American cemeteries remind us of the young boys who never made it home, and whose memory we cherish. My generation does not own this   freedom; we are merely its custodians.   We   can only hand over this hard won liberty to   Europe 's children in the same state in which it was offered to us. We cannot strike a deal with mullahs and imams.   Future generations   would never forgive us. We cannot squander our liberties. We simply do not have the right to do so.

We have to   take the necessary action now to stop this Islamic stupidity from destroying the free world that we know.

****

One of the hardest questions to answer is why their "spiritual" leaders demand that infidels be killed. Following is a recent statement:

**

White House spokesman Robert Gibbs says the U.S. government is actively pursuing American-born terrorist Anwar al-Awlaki.

White House Press Secretary Robert Gibbs says the Obama administration is making every effort to track down <u>American-born</u> Anwar al-Awlaki, who is reportedly hiding in a remote mountainous region of Yemen's

Shabwa Province.

"We are actively trying to find him and many others throughout the world that seek to do our country, and to do our interests, great harm," Gibbs said.

Al-Awlaki, who is the son of a prominent Yemeni politician, is calling for the killing of American citizens in a new video posted Sunday on the internet.   The Yemeni branch of a group that calls itself al-Qaida in the Arabian Peninsula released the video.

Speaking on the CBS television news' "Face the Nation" program, Gibbs says al-Awlaki advocates killing and violence.

"···despite telling the world that he is a cleric, you see on a video tape that he supports al-Qaida's agenda of murder and violence," Gibbs said. "In fact, in recent video tapes, he has said he is a member of al-Qaida in the Arabian peninsula, who has an agenda just like al-Qaida to strike targets in Yemen, throughout the world, including here in the United States."

Gibbs also lashed out at al-Qaida, repeating President Barack Obama's description of the group to graduating cadets at the U.S. Military Academy, Saturday.

"The president said ... that members of al Qaida are small men who will be on the wrong side of history," Gibbs said. "Those cadets, many of (whom) will go to Afghanistan to pursue our battles there to keep our country safe and the president will continue to take action directly at terrorists like Awlaki and keep our country safe from their murderous thugs."

Al-Awlaki is alleged to have been a mentor

of Fort Hood shooter, Major Nidal Malak Hasan, who killed 13 people at the Texas base. He is also alleged to have been in contact with Umar Farouk Abdulmutallab, who tried unsuccessfully to blow up a Detroit-bound airliner on Christmas Day.

****

Talking about bombers, here is something you probably haven't heard much about since he tried to blow up an airplane with a bomb planted in his shoe. The words the judge used to sentence Richard Reid needs to be memorized by all school children and to think the newspapers didn't say a word.

**

Remember the guy who got on a plane with a bomb built into his shoe and tried to light it?

Did you know his trial is over?
Did you know he was sentenced?
Did you see/hear any of the judge's comments on TV or Radio?
Didn't think so.!!!

Everyone should hear what the judge had to say.

Ruling by Judge William Young, US District Court.

Prior to sentencing, the Judge asked the defendant if he had anything to say. His response: After admitting his guilt to the court for the record, Reid also admitted his 'allegiance to Osama bin Laden, to Islam, and to the religion of Allah,' defiantly stating, 'I think I will not apologize for my actions,' and told the court 'I am at war with your country.'

Judge Young then delivered the statement quoted below:

January 30, 2003, United States vs. Reid. Judge Young: 'Mr. Richard C. Reid, hearken now to the sentence the Court imposes upon you.

On counts 1, 5 and 6 the Court sentences you to life in prison in the custody of the United States Attorney General. On counts 2, 3, 4 and 7, the Court sentences you to 20 years in prison on each count, the sentence on each count to run consecutively.. (That's 80 years.)

On count 8 the Court sentences you to the mandatory 30 years again, to be served consecutively to the 80 years just imposed. The Court imposes upon you for each of the eight counts a fine of $250,000

that's an aggregate fine of $2 million.
The Court accepts the government's
recommendation with respect to restitution and orders restitution in the amount
of $298.17 to Andre Bousquet and $5,784
to American Airlines.

The Court imposes upon you an $800
special assessment. The Court imposes
upon you five years supervised release
simply because the law requires it. But
the life sentences are real life sentences
so I need go no further.

This is the sentence that is provided for
by our statutes. It is a fair and just
sentence. It is a righteous sentence.

Now, let me explain this to you. We are
not afraid of you or any of your terrorist
co-conspirators, Mr. Reid. We are
Americans. We have been through the

fire before. There is too much war talk here and I say that to everyone with the utmost respect. Here in this court, we deal with individuals as individuals and care for individuals as individuals. As human beings, we reach out for justice.

You are not an enemy combatant. You are a terrorist. You are not a soldier in any war. You are a terrorist. To give you that reference, to call you a soldier, gives you far too much stature. Whether the officers of government do it or your attorney does it, or if you think you are a soldier, you are not----- you are a terrorist. And we do not negotiate with terrorists. We do not meet with terrorists. We do not sign documents with terrorists. We hunt them down one by one and bring them to justice.

So war talk is way out of line in this court. You are a big fellow. But you are not that big. You're no warrior. I've known warriors. You are a terrorist. A species of criminal that is guilty of multiple attempted murders. In a very real sense, State Trooper Santiago had it right when you first were taken off that plane and into custody and you wondered where the press and the TV crews were, and he said: 'You're no big deal.'

You are no big deal.

What your able counsel and what the equally able United States attorneys have grappled with and what I have as honestly as I know how tried to grapple with, is why you did something so horrific. What was it that led you here to this courtroom today?

I have listened respectfully to what you have to say. And I ask you to search your heart and ask yourself what sort of unfathomable hate led you to do what you are guilty and admit you are guilty of doing? And, I have an answer for you. It may not satisfy you, but as I search this entire record, it comes as close to understanding as I know.

It seems to me you hate the one thing that to us is most precious. You hate our freedom. Our individual freedom. Our individual freedom to live as we choose, to come and go as we choose, to believe or not believe as we individually choose. Here, in this society, the very wind carries freedom. It carries it everywhere from sea to shining sea. It is because we prize individual freedom so much that you are here in this beautiful courtroom, so that everyone can see, truly see, that justice is administered fairly, individually, and discretely. It is for freedom's sake that your lawyers are striving so vigorously on your behalf, have filed appeals, will go on in their representation of you before other judges.

We Americans are all about freedom. Because we all know that the way we treat you, Mr. Reid, is the measure of our own liberties. Make no mistake though. It is yet true that we will bear any burden; pay any price, to preserve our freedoms. Look around this courtroom. Mark it well. The world is not going to long remember what you or I say here. The day after tomorrow, it will be forgotten, but this, however, will long endure.

Here in this courtroom and courtrooms
all across America , the American people will gather to see that justice, individual justice, justice, not war, individual
justice is in fact being done. The very
President of the United States through his
officers will have to come
into courtrooms and lay out evidence
on which specific matters can be
judged and juries of citizens will gather
to sit and judge that evidence demo-
cratically, to mold and shape and refine
our sense of justice..

See that flag, Mr. Reid? That's the flag of
the United States of America . That flag
will fly there long after this is all forgotten.
That flag stands for freedom. And it always will.   Mr. Custody Officer. Stand
him down.

So, how much of this Judge's comments did we hear on our TV sets? We need more judges like Judge Young. Powerful words that strike home.

****

Recently, the word "profiling" has been looked down upon because it seemed to represent taking away some of our freedoms. Those that don't like profiling, please read the following:

**

WE HAVE TO BELIEVE AND BEGIN TO DO SOMETHING OR WE ALL WILL LOOSE OUR COUNTRY AS WE KNOW IT TODAY, IN THE NOT TO DISTANT FUTURE.
I DON'T KNOW ABOUT YOU ALL BUT I AM SICK AND TIRED OF ALL THIS POLITICALLY CORRECT CRAP.

THEY ARE OUT TO KILL US AND TAKE CONTROL OF OUR LIBERTIES AND MOST IMPORTANTLY OUR FREEDOM!!!!!!!

A lot of Americans have become so insulated from reality...
Absolutely No Profiling! Pause a moment, reflect back, and
take the following multiple choice test.

These events are actual events from history.. They really happened! Do you remember?

HERE'S THE TEST

1. 1968 Bobby Kennedy was shot and killed by:

a.. Superman

b. Jay Leno

c. Harry Potter

d. A Muslim male extremist between the ages of 17 and 40

2. In 1972 at the Munich Olympics, athletes were kidnapped and massacred by :

a. Olga Corbett

b. Sitting Bull

c. Arnold Schwarzenegger

d. Muslim male extremists mostly between the ages of 17 and 40

3. In 1979, the US embassy in Iran was taken over by:

a. Lost Norwegians

b. Elvis

c. A tour bus full of 80-year-old women

d . Muslim male extremists mostly between the ages of 17 and 40

4. During the 1980's a number of Americans were kidnapped in Lebanon by:

a. John Dillinger

b. The King of Sweden

c. The Boy Scouts

d. Muslim male extremists mostly between the ages of 17 and 40

5. In 1983, the US Marine barracks in Beirut was blown up by:

a. A pizza delivery boy

b. Pee Wee Herman

c.. Geraldo Rivera

d. Muslim male extremists mostly between the ages of 17 and 40

6. In 1985 the cruise ship Achille Lauro
was hijacked and a 70 year old American passenger was murdered and
thrown overboard in his wheelchair by:

a. The Smurfs

b. Davey Jones

c. The Little Mermaid

d. Muslim male extremists mostly between the ages of 17 and 40

7. In 1985 TWA flight 847 was hijacked
at Athens , and a US Navy diver trying to
rescue passengers was murdered by:

a. Captain Kidd

b. Charles Lindberg

c. Mother Teresa

d. Muslim male extremists mostly between the ages of 17 and 40

8. In 1988, Pan Am Flight 103 was bombed by:

a. Scooby Doo

b. The Tooth Fairy

c. The Sundance Kid

d. Muslim male extremists mostly between the ages of 17 and 40

9. In 1993 the World Trade Center was bombed the first time by:

a. Richard Simmons

b. Grandma Moses

c. Michael Jordan

d. Muslim male extremists mostly between the ages of 17 and 40

10. In 1998, the US embassies in Kenya
and Tanzania were bombed by:

a. Mr. Rogers

b. Hillary Clinton, to distract attention
from Wild Bill's women problems

c. The World Wrestling Federation

d. Muslim male extremists mostly between the ages of 17 and 40

11. On 9/11/01, four airliners were hijacked; two were used as missiles to take
out the World Trade Centers and of the
remaining two, one crashed into the US
Pentagon and the other was diverted
and crashed by the passengers.

Thousands of people were killed by:

a. Bugs Bunny, Wiley E. Coyote, Daffy Duck and Elmer Fudd

b. The Supreme Court of Florida

c. Mr Bean

d. Muslim male extremists mostly between the ages of 17 and 40

12. In 2002 the United States fought a war in Afghanistan against:

a. Enron

b. The Lutheran Church

c. The NFL

d. Muslim male extremists mostly between the ages of 17 and 40

13. In 2002 reporter Daniel Pearl was kidnapped and murdered by:

a. Bonnie and Clyde

b. Captain Kangaroo

c. Billy Graham

d. Muslim male extremists mostly between the ages of 17 and 40

No, I really don't see a pattern here to justify profiling, do you? So, to ensure we Americans never offend anyone, particularly fanatics intent on killing us, airport security screeners will no longer be allowed to profile certain people.. They must conduct random searches of 80-year-old women, little kids, airline pilots with proper identification, secret agents who are members of the President's security detail, 85-year old Congressmen with metal hips, and Medal of Honor winner and former Governor Joe Foss, but leave Muslim Males between the ages 17 and 40 alone lest they be guilty of profiling.

Foot note: Fort Hood Texas ......another Muslim 39 years old killed 13 people and wounded 30 some odd others... Does this fit the profile!

NOW OUR COMMANDER-IN-CHIEF IS TELLING EVERYONE
THAT THE YOUNG MUSLIM THAT AT-TEMPTED TO BLOW UP A NORTHWEST/ DELTA JET AS IT APPROACHED DETROIT ON CHRISTMAS DAY WAS (QUOTE) "AN ISOLATED INCIDENT".
YOU HAVE GOT TO BE SHITTING ME OR WHAT!!! MY FATHER
USED TO SAY: "PLEASE DON'T PISS ON MY LEG AND TELL
ME IT'S RAINING."

****

Generally when people get to be 60 plus, they pretty well know the score. Robert A. Hall, who is 63 has written an article about what he doesn't like to hear. He's tired of listening to all the BS distributed by our government and wants to set the record straight:

**

I'm tired of being told that Islam is a "Religion of Peace," when every day I can read dozens of stories of Muslim men killing their sisters, wives and daughters for their family "honor"; of Muslims rioting over some slight offense; of Muslims murdering Christian and Jews because they aren't "believers"; of Muslims burning schools for girls; of Muslims stoning teenage rape victims to death for "adultery"; of Muslims mutilating the genitals of little girls; all in the name of Allah, because the Qur'an and Shari'a law tells them to.

****

More from his article later. This profiling thing is affecting many people in many walks of life. An airline pilot with American Airlines wrote this article:

**

The paper stated today that some Muslim doctor is saying we are profiling him because he has been checked three times while getting on an airplane.

The following is a letter from a pilot. This well spoken man, who is a pilot with American Airlines, says what is in his heart, beautifully.... Read, absorb and pass this on.

'YOU WORRY ME!' By American Airlines Pilot - Captain John Maniscalco

I've been trying to say this since 911, but you worry me. I wish you didn't. I wish when I walked down the streets of this country that I love, that your color and culture still blended with the beautiful human landscape we enjoy in this country. But you don't blend in anymore. I notice you, and it worries me.

I notice you because I can't help it anymore. People from your homelands, pro-
fessing to be Muslims, have been attack-
ing and killing my fellow citizens and our
friends for more than 20 years now. I
don't fully understand their grievances
and hate, but I know that nothing can
justify the inhumanity of their attacks.

On September 11, ARAB-MUSLIMS hijacked four jetliners in my country. They
cut the throats of women in front of children and brutally stabbed to death others. They took control of those planes
and crashed them into buildings killing
thousands of proud fathers, loving sons,
wise grandparents, elegant daughters,
best friends, favorite coaches, fearless
public servants, and children's mothers.

The Palestinians celebrated, the Iraqis
were overjoyed as was most of the Arab
world. So, I notice you now. I don't want
to be worried. I don't want to be con-
sumed by the same rage and hate and
prejudice that has destroyed the soul of
these terrorists But I need your help. As

a rational American, trying to protect my country and family in an irrational and unsafe world, I must know how to tell the difference between you, and the Arab/ Muslim terrorist.

How do I differentiate between the true Arab/Muslim Americans and the Arab/ Muslim terrorists in our communities who are attending our schools, enjoying our parks, and living in OUR communities under the protection of OUR constitution, while they plot the next attack that will slaughter these same good neighbors and children?

The events of September 11th changed the answer. It is not my responsibility to determine which of you embraces our great country, with ALL of its religions, with ALL of its different citizens, with all of its faults. It is time for every Arab/Muslim in this country to determine it for me.

I want to know, I demand to know, and I have a right to know, whether or not you love America. Do you pledge allegiance to its flag? Do you proudly display it in front of your house, or on your car? Do you pray in your many daily prayers that Allah will bless this nation, that He will protect and prosper it? Or do you pray that Allah with destroy it in one of your Jihad's? Are you thankful for the freedom that only this nation affords? A freedom that was paid for by the blood of hundreds of thousands of patriots who gave their lives for this country? Are you willing to preserve this freedom by also paying the ultimate sacrifice? Do you love America ? If this is your commitment, then I need YOU to start letting ME know about it.

Your Muslim leaders in this nation should be flooding the media at this time with hard facts on your faith, and what hard actions you are taking as a community and as a religion to protect the United States of America. Please, no more benign overtures of regret for the death of the innocent because I worry about who you regard as innocent. No more benign overtures of condemnation for the unprovoked attacks because I worry about what is unprovoked to you. I am not interested in any more sympathy. I am only interested in action. What will you do for America - our great country - at this time of crisis, at this time of war?

I want to see Arab-Muslims waving the AMERICAN flag in the streets. I want to hear you chanting 'Allah Bless America ' I want to see young Arab/Muslim men enlisting in the military. I want to see a commitment of money, time, and emotion to the victims of this butchering and to this nation as a whole.

The FBI has a list of over 400 people they want to talk to regarding the WTC attack. Many of these people live and socialize right now in Muslim communities. You know them. You know where they are. Hand them over to us, now! But I have seen little even approaching this sort of action. Instead I have seen an already closed and secretive community close even tighter. You have disappeared from the streets. You have posted armed security guards at your facilities. You have threatened lawsuits. You have screamed for protection from reprisals.

The very few Arab/Muslim representatives that HAVE appeared in the media were defensive and equivocating. They seemed more concerned with making sure that the United States proves who was responsible before taking action. They seemed more concerned with protecting their fellow Muslims from violence directed towards them in the United States and abroad than they did with supporting our country and denouncing 'leaders' like Khadafi, Hussein, Farrakhan, and Arafat.

If the true teachings of Islam proclaim tolerance and peace and love for all people, then I want chapter and verse from the Koran and statements from popular Muslim leaders to back it up. What good is it if the teachings in the Koran are good, and pure, and true, when your 'leaders' are teaching fanatical in-

terpretations, terrorism, and intoler-
ance? It matters little how good Islam
SHOULD BE if huge numbers of the
world's Muslims interpret the teachings of
Mohammed incorrectly and adhere to a
degenerative form of the religion. A
form that has been demonstrated to us
over and over again. A form whose s-
tructure is built upon a foundation of violence, death, and suicide. A form
whose members are recruited from the
prisons around the world. A form whose
members (some as young as five years
old) are seen day after day, week in and
week out, year after year, marching in
the streets around the world, burning ef-
figies of our presidents, burning the
American flag, shooting weapons into
the air. A form whose members convert
from a peaceful religion, only to take up
arms against the great United States of
America, the country of their birth. A
form whose rules are so twisted, that their
traveling members refuse to show their
faces at airport security checkpoints, in
the name of Islam. We will NEVER allow
the attacks of September 11, or any oth-

ers for that matter, to take away that which is so precious to us: Our rights under the greatest constitution in the world. I want to know where every Arab Muslim in this country stands and I think it is my right and the right of every true citizen of this country to demand it. A right paid for by the blood of thousands of my brothers and sisters who died protecting the very constitution that is protecting you and your family. I am pleading with you to let me know. I want you here as my brother, my neighbor, my friend, as a fellow American. But there can be no gray areas or ambivalence regarding your allegiance, and it is up to YOU, to show ME, where YOU stand. Until then. 'YOU WORRY ME!'

I totally agree with this sentiment. I hope you will forget all about the 'political correctness' mandate we've had rammed down our throats, and see if this doesn't ring true in your heart and mind.
For Canada, with all the multiculturism we've been told is so important....why should we not, as Canadians, expect

that the millions of new people immigrating to our country will show their love for our country, their allegiance to our country, their willingness to obey the laws of our country, and acceptance that we are a Christian country? Just because they are able to enjoy exercising their own religion, they should not expect us to be ashamed of ours. They
knew Canada was a Christian country when they came here. Why are we erasing Christianity because immigrants who are unwilling to adopt our way of life expect us to? There is just too much insanity in the world, and we have to start taking a stand. I hope you will forward, so others will feel they are not alone if they are starting to feel the same. ashamed of ours. They knew Canada was a Christian country when they came here. Why are we erasing Christianity because immigrants who are unwilling to adopt our way of life expect us to? There is just too much insanity in the world, and we have to start taking a stand. I hope you will forward, so others will feel they are not

alone if they are starting to feel the same.

****

As you may or may not know, Arab women are treated like dirt. The following is an article from an Arab woman from Egypt showing exactly how the Arab women live:

**

This was written by a woman born in Egypt as a Muslim. This is not hearsay.

Joys of Muslim Women
by Nonie Darwish

_____

In the Muslim faith a Muslim man can marry a child as young as 1 year old and have sexual intimacy with this child. Consummating the marriage by 9.

The dowry is given to the family in exchange for the woman (who becomes his slave) and for the purchase of the private parts of the woman, to use her as a toy.

Even though a woman is abused she can not obtain a divorce.

To prove rape, the woman must have (4) male witnesses.

Often after a woman has been raped, she is returned to her family and the family must return the dowry. The family has the right to execute her (an honor killing) to restore the honor of the family. Husbands can beat their wives 'at will' and he does not have to say why he has beaten her.

The husband is permitted to have (4 wives) and a temporary wife for an hour (prostitute) at his discretion.. The Shariah Muslim law controls the private as well as the public life of the woman.

In the West World (America) Muslim men are starting to demand Shariah Law so the wife can not obtain a divorce and he can have full and complete control of her. It is amazing and alarming how many of our sisters and daughters attending American Universities are now marrying Muslim men and submitting themselves and their children unsuspectingly to the Shariah law.

By passing this on, enlightened American women may avoid becoming a slave under Shariah Law.

Ripping the West in Two.

Author and lecturer Nonie Darwish says the goal of radical Islamists is to impose Shariah law on the world, ripping Western law and liberty in two.

She recently authored the book, Cruel and Usual Punishment: The Terrifying Global Implications of Islamic Law.

Darwish was born in Cairo and spent her childhood in Egypt and Gaza before immigrating to America in 1978, when she was eight years old. Her father died while leading covert attacks on Israel . He was a high-ranking Egyptian military officer stationed with his family in Gaza .

When he died, he was considered a "shahid," a martyr for jihad. His posthumous status earned Nonie and her family an elevated position in Muslim society.

But Darwish developed a skeptical eye at an early age. She questioned her own Muslim culture and upbringing. She converted to Christianity after hearing a Christian preacher on television.

In her latest book, Darwish warns about creeping sharia law - what it is, what it means, and how it is manifested in Islamic countries. For the West, she says radical Islamists are working to impose sharia on the world. If that happens, Western civilization will be destroyed. Westerners generally assume all religions encourage a respect for the dignity of each individual. Islamic law (Sharia) teaches that non-Muslims should be subjugated or killed in this world.

Peace and prosperity for one's children is not as important as assuring that Islamic law rules everywhere in the Middle East and eventually in the world.

While Westerners tend to think that all re-ligions encourage some form of the golden rule, Sharia teaches two systems of ethics - one for Muslims and another for non-Muslims. Building on tribal prac-tices of the seventh century, Sharia en-courages the side of humanity that wants to take from and subjugate others.

While Westerners tend to think in terms of religious people developing a personal understanding of and relationship with God, Sharia advocates executing peo-ple who ask difficult questions that could be interpreted as criticism.

It's hard to imagine, that in this day and age, Islamic scholars agree that those who criticize Islam or choose to stop being Muslim should be executed. Sadly, while talk of an Islamic reformation is common and even assumed by many in the West, such murmurings in the Middle East are silenced through intimidation.

While Westerners are accustomed to an increase in religious tolerance over time, Darwish explains how petro dollars are being used to grow an extremely intolerant form of political Islam in her native Egypt and elsewhere.

In twenty years there will be enough Muslim voters in the U.S. to elect the President by themselves! Rest assured they will do so... You can look at how they have taken over several towns in the USA .. Dearborn Mich. is one... and there are others...

I think everyone in the U.S. should be required to read this, but with the ACLU,

Ron Berger   86

there is no way this will be widely publicized, unless each of us sends it on!

It is too bad that so many are disillusioned with life and Christianity to accept Muslims as peaceful.. some may be but they have an army that is willing to shed blood in the name of Islam.. the peaceful support the warriors with their finances and own kind of patriotism to their religion. <u>While America is getting rid of Christianity from all public sites and erasing God from the lives of children the Muslims are planning a great jihad on America ..</u>

This is your chance to make a difference... Pass it on to your email list or at least those you think will listen..

****

Did you ever hear of dhimmitude? I didn't either until I received this email. Once you are conquered through jihad they either kill you or tax you and use you like slaves.

**

Dhimmitude is the Muslim system of controlling non-muslim populations conquered through jihad. Specifically, it is the TAXING of non-muslims in exchange for tolerating their presence AND as a coercive means of converting conquered remnants to islam.

The ObamaCare bill is the establishment of Dhimmitude and Sharia muslim diktat in the United States . Muslims are specifically exempted from the government mandate to purchase insurance, and also from the penalty tax for being uninsured. Islam considers insurance to be "gambling", "risk-taking" and "usury" and is thus banned. Muslims are specifically granted exemption based on this. How convenient. So I, Ann Barnhardt, a Christian, will have crippling IRS liens placed against all of my assets, including real estate, cattle, and even accounts receivables, and will face hard prison time because I refuse to buy insurance or pay the penalty tax. Meanwhile, Louis Farrakhan will have no such penalty and will have 100% of his health needs paid for by the de facto government insurance. Non-muslims will be paying a tax to subsidize muslims. Period. This is Dhimmitude.

Dhimmitude serves two purposes: it enriches the muslim masters AND serves to drive conversions to islam. In this case, the incentive to convert to islam will be taken up by those in the inner-cities as well as the godless Generation X, Y and Z types who have no moral anchor. If you don't believe in Christ to begin with, it is no problem whatsoever to sell Him for 30 pieces of silver. "Sure, I'll be a muslim if it means free health insurance and no taxes. Where do I sign, bro?"

****

BRITISH SURVEY

A recent survey in the United Kingdom asked the following question:

Are there too many foreigners in this country now?

Answer:

18% said: YES

82% said: معهد الأمن العالمي بوا شنط

FRIENDS OF IRONY

Maybe you don't believe that Muslim countries line up against us. It has been happening for quite some time now and it will get worse as time goes along. I believe that the question of should we get out of the UN be brought up again or should we just shut these countries off and try and get along with the others?

I know that most of you know very little about how much aid we give these countries that vote against us the majority of times. This email should open your eyes.

Try and imagine that during WW-11 we fought the Germans, Italians and Japanese at the same time we gave them money in aid. Doesn't make a whole lot of sense, does it? It doesn't make any more sense today.

**

This will make your hair curl !

How they vote in the United Nations:

Below are the actual voting records of various Arabic/Islamic States which are recorded in both the US State Department and United Nations records:

Kuwait votes against the United States 67% of the time

Qatar votes against the United States 67% of the time

Morocco votes against the United States 70% of the time

United Arab Emirates votes against the U. S. 70% of the time.

Jordan votes against the United States 71% of the time.

Tunisia votes against the United States 71% of the time.

Saudi Arabia votes against the United States 73% of the time.

Yemen votes against the United States 74% of the time.

Algeria votes against the United States 74% of the time.

Oman votes against the United States 74% of the time.

Sudan votes against the United States 75% of the time.

Pakistan votes against the United States 75% of the time.

Libya votes against the United States 76% of the time.

Egypt votes against the   United States 79% of the time.

Lebanon votes against the United States 80% of the time.

India votes against the United States 81% of the time.

Syria votes against the   United States 84% of the time.

Mauritania votes against the   United States 87% of the time.

U S Foreign Aid to those that hate us:

Egypt, for example, after voting 79% of the time against the United States, still receives $2 billion annually in US Foreign Aid.

Jordan votes 71% against the United States

And receives $192,814,000 annually in US Foreign Aid.

Pakistan votes 75% against the United States

Receives $6,721,000 annually in US Foreign Aid.

India votes 81% against the United States

Receives $143,699,000 annually.

Perhaps it is time to get out of the UN and give the tax savings back to the American workers who are having to skimp and sacrifice to pay the taxes (and gasoline).

Disgusting isn't it?

****

I sure hope you have had a chance to understand how serious this all is. We do not have time to waste - we must act NOW.

**

IN CASE YOU HAVE NOT SEEN THIS.

READ CAREFULLY...........

This is so "Unbelievable"....
In Houston ...

Harwin Central Mall: The very first store that you come to when you walk from the lobby of the building into the shopping area had this sign posted on their door. The shop is run by Muslims.
Feel free to share this with others.

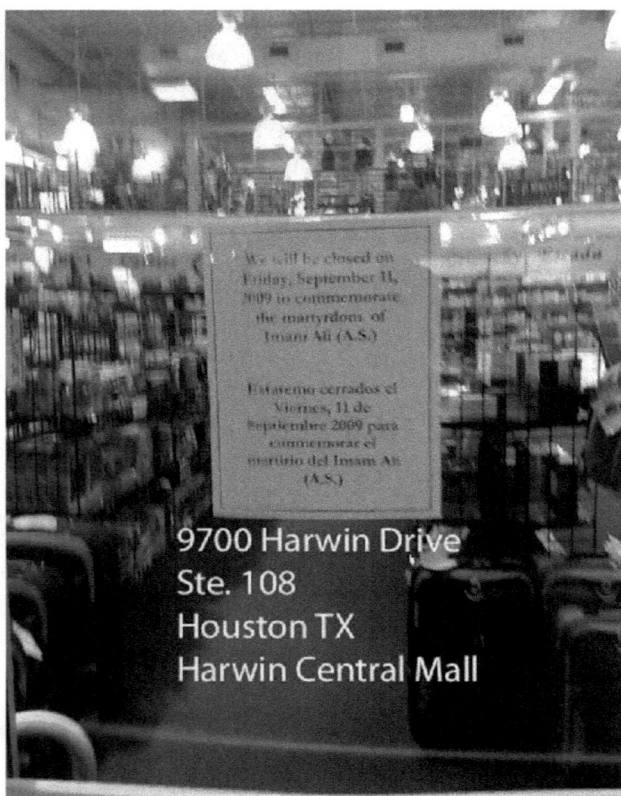

We will be closed on
Friday, September 11,
2009 to commemorate
the martyrdom of
Imam Ali (A.S.)

Estaremo cerrados el
Viernes, 11 de
Septiembre 2009 para
commemorar el
martirio del Imam Ali
(A.S.)

9700 Harwin Drive
Ste. 108
Houston TX
Harwin Central Mall

Imam Ali flew one of the planes into
the twin towers.

Nice huh?

Try telling me we're not in a Religious
war!

****

Before I leave this segment, I wish to let you know a little about the terrorist organizations in the world. We've only heard of a few of them, but there are many that are bent on destroying our way of life.

There are at least 82 different terrorist organizations that are known. They start with <u>Abu Nidal Organization (ANO)</u> (Fatah Revolutionary Council, Arab Revolutionary Brigades, Black September, and Revolutionary Organization of Socialist Muslims) down through <u>Zapatista National Liberation Army (EZLN)</u> which is in Mexico.

The major one that we know something about is <u>al-Qaeda</u> (The Base, Qa'idat al-Jihad, Islamic Army for the Liberation of the Holy Places, World Islamic Front for Jihad Against Jews and Crusaders, Islamic Salvation Foundation, Osama bin Laden Network).

Here is a statement that is sure to make your hair curl: Department of Homeland Security Secretary Janet Napolitano,(editor's note from

Jane: Napolitano: aka "Sleepy") testifying at a Senate Judiciary Committee meeting, said the southern border in Arizona is as safe as it ever has been. Now that she said it was safe - I guess it is.

I'm sure you can see that there is a massive effort out there to disrupt our way of life. I'm sure you can also see that the people we have in charge to prevent that are really not up to the task. You don't hire a politician to do a policeman's job.

I wish to throw in another "tid-bit" for those that really believe that their "clerics" are "religious". This is a typical statement from their religious leaders that want the world to know they are peaceful:

**

A radical U.S.-born Muslim cleric is urging Muslims serving in the U.S. Army to kill American soldiers in Afghanistan and Iraq.

In a video posted Sunday on Islamist militant websites, Anwar al-Awlaki said he justifies the deaths of U.S. soldiers because Americans have intentionally killed what he said were millions of Muslim civilians in Afghanistan and Iraq.

He also praised U.S. Army Major Nidal Hasan, who is accused of killing 13 people last year at Fort Hood, a U.S. military base in the southern state of Texas. He said in the video that Hasan performed a "heroic act."

Last month, U.S. officials said the Obama administration had authorized the CIA to capture or kill Awlaki, an al-Qaida operative born in the U.S. to Yemeni parents.

Awlaki is believed to be hiding in a mountainous region in southeastern Yemen's Shabwa province.

Yemen intensified its campaign against al-Qaida militants after the group's local branch, al-Qaida in the Arabian Peninsula, claimed responsibility for the failed bombing of a U.S.-bound passenger jet last December.

****

While so much talk has been on terror to our land, we can't forget about the Jews that feel this terror almost every day. The Muslims feel they are owed so much, but have contributed so little in the way of improving the world. Here is a comparison as to the contributions made by both the Jews and Muslims:

**

DIFFERENCES BETWEEN JEWS AND MUS-LIMS

Interesting Perspective on The Difference Between
Jews and Muslims

And the Muslims want to wipe the Jews off the face of the earth -- wow, what a difference that would make...........

DIFFERENCES BETWEEN JEWS AND MUS-LIMS. I thought you
would be interested in reading this....(What a contrast!)

Ron Berger   100

How could the picture be 'painted' any more vividly?

The Global Islamic population is approximately 1,200,000,000
ONE BILLION TWO HUNDRED MILLION or 20% of the world's population.

They have received the following Nobel Prizes:

Literature:
1988 - Najib Mahfooz

Peace:

1978 - Mohamed Anwar El-Sadat
1990 - Elias James Corey
1994 - Yaser Arafat:
1999 - Ahmed Zewai

Economics:
(zero)

Physics:

(zero)

Medicine:
1960 - Peter Brian Medawar
1998 - Ferid Mourad

TOTAL: 7 SEVEN ONLY

>>>>>>>>>>>>>>>>>>>>>>>>>>>>>>>>>>>>

The Global Jewish population is approximately 14,000,000
Only FOURTEEN MILLION or about 0.02%
of the world's population.

They have received the following Nobel
Prizes:

Literature:

1910 - Paul Heyse
1927 - Henri Bergson
1958 - Boris Pasternak
1966 - Shmuel Yosef Agnon
1966 - Nelly Sachs
1976 - Saul Bellow
1978 - Isaac Bashevis Singer

1981 - Elias Canetti
1987 - Joseph Brodsky
1991 - Nadine Gordimer World

Peace:

1911 - Alfred Fried
1911 - Tobias Michael Carel Asser
1968 - Rene Cassin
1973 - Henry Kissinger
1978 - Menachem Begin
1986 - Elie Wiesel
1994 - Shimon Peres
1994 - Yitzhak Rabin

Physics:

1905 - Adolph Von Baeyer
1906 - Henri Moissan
1907 - Albert Abraham Michelson
1908 - Gabriel Lippmann
1910 - Otto Wallach
1915 - Richard Willstaetter
1918 - Fritz Haber
1921 - Albert Einstein
1922 - Niels Bohr
1925 - James Franck

1925 - Gustav Hertz
1943 - Gustav Stern
1943 - George Charles de Hevesy
1944 - Isidor Issac Rabi
1952 - Felix Bloch
1954 - Max Born
1958 - Igor Tamm
1959 - Emilio Segre
1960 - Donald A. Glaser
1961 - Robert Hofstadter
1961 - Melvin Calvin
196 2 - Lev Davidovich Landau
1962 - Max Ferdinand Perutz
1965 - Richard Phillips Feynman
1965 - Julian Schwinger
1969 - Murray Gell-Mann
1971 - Dennis Gabor
1972 - William Howard Stein
1973 - Brian David Josephson
1975 - Benjamin Mottleson
1976 - Burton Richter
1977 - Ilya Prigogine
1978 - Arno Allan Penzias
1978 - P eter L Kapitza
1979 - Stephen Weinberg
1979 - Sheldon Glashow
1979 - Herbert Charles Brown

1980 - Paul Berg
1980 - Walter Gilbert
1981 - Roald Hoffmann
1982 - Aaron Klug
1985 - Albert A. Hauptman
1985 - Jerome Karle
1986 - Dudley R. Herschbach
1988 - Robert Huber
1988 - Leon Lederman
1988 - Melvin Schwartz
1988 - Jack Steinberger
1989 - Sidney Altman
1990 - Jerome Friedman
1992 - Rudolph Marcus
1995 - Martin Perl
2000 - Alan J. Heeger

Economics:

1970 - Paul Anthony Samuelson
1971 - Simon Kuznets
1972 - Kenneth Joseph Arrow
1975 - Leonid Kantorovich
1976 - Milton Friedman
1978 - Herbert A. Simon
1980 - Lawrence Robert Klein
1985 - Franco Modigliani

1987 - Robert M. Solow
1990 - Harry Markowitz
1990 - Merton Miller
1992 - Gary Becker
1993 - Robert Fogel

Medicine:

1908 - Elie Metchnikoff
1908 - Paul Erlich
1914 - Robert Barany
1922 - Otto Meyerhof
1930 - Karl Landsteiner
1931 - Otto Warburg
1936 - Otto Loewi
1944 - Joseph Erlanger
1944 - Herb ert Spencer Gasser
1945 - Ernst Boris Chain
1946 - Hermann Joseph Muller
1950 - Tadeus Reichstein
1952 - Selman AbrahamWaksman
1953 - Hans Krebs
1953 - Fritz Albert Lipmann
1958 - Joshua Lederberg
1959 - Arthur Kornberg
1964 - Konrad Bloch
1965 - Francois Jacob

1965 - Andre Lwoff
1967 - George Wald
1968 - Marshall W. Nirenberg
1969 - Salvador Luria
1970 - Julius Axelrod
1970 - Sir Bernard Katz
1972 - Gerald Maurice Edelman
1975 - Howard Martin Temin
1976 - Baruch S. Blumberg
1977 - Roselyn Sussman Yalow
1978 - Daniel Nathans
1980 - Baruj Benacerraf
1984 - Cesar Milstein
1985 - Michael Stuart Brown
1985 - Joseph L. Goldstein
1986 - Stanley Cohen [& Rita Levi-
        Montalcini]
1988 - Gertrude Elion
1989 - Harold Varmus
1991 - Erwin Neher
1991 - Bert Sakmann
1993 - Richard J. Roberts
1993 - Phillip Sharp
1994 - Alfred Gilman
1995 - Edward B. Lewis

TOTAL: 129 ONE HUNDRED TWENTY NINE!

The Jews are NOT promoting brain washing children in military training camps, teaching them how to blow themselves up and cause maximum deaths of Jews and other non Muslims!

The Jews don't hijack planes, nor kill athletes at the Olympics, or blow themselves up in German restaurants. There is NOT one single Jew that has destroyed a church. There is NOT a single Jew that protests by killing people.

The Jews don't traffic slaves, nor have leaders calling for Jihad and death to all the Infidels.

Perhaps the world's Muslims should consider investing more in standard education and less in blaming the Jews for all their problems.

Muslims must ask 'what can they do for humankind' before they demand that humankind respects them!!

Regardless of your feelings about the crisis between Israel and the Palestinians and Arab neighbors, even if you believe there is more culpability on Israel's part, the following two sentences really say it all:

'If the Arabs put down their weapons today, there would be no more violence. If the Jews put down their weapons today, there would be no more Israel'.

-Benjamin Netanyahu

****

Wake up America - The fox is guarding the hen house.

Lest we forget -

September 11, 2001

MEXICO

Our Enemy to the South

Yes, this is the same Mexico that you drive to for cheap wrought iron, statues, clothes and a myriad of other items. It's also the place where you can see mothers breast feeding their young on the public streets while holding their hand out for donations. This is also the place where you are afraid to get out of your vehicle for fear of getting mugged or attacked and not only by criminals, but by the police.

Try getting back across the border without someone washing your windshield and then demanding money for their efforts.

Some people don't seem to have a problem. I've only been to Mexico three times. Once in 1958 when I was too naive to understand things, once on a "Mexican Riviera" cruise and once while visiting San Diego we ventured across to border, but never got out of the car and came right back across to the US.

Don't get me wrong. I've known a lot of Mexicans and had no problem working with them. Construction became "heavy" with Mexicans early in my career. Most started in the landscape business, but soon many became carpenters and painters, roofers and drywallers, plus many other trades. Most worked very hard and many did very acceptable work.

I had a great experience with the landscaping crew that we usually had. Most of the workers wanted to do a good job for you and actually delighted in pleasing you. One worker went back to Mexico one weekend and was stopped by the police. He had forgotten that he had a gun in the glove compartment and the police threw him in jail. After several weeks they released him, but under the conditions that he pay a fine and report back every two weeks and sign in. The problem with that was that the place to sign in was a twelve hour bus ride every time. This went on for several years.

I am not talking about those that crossed the border to make a better life for themselves, but those that come across for all the benefits and contribute nothing except to the crime statistics. Expectant mothers race across the border just to have their baby. Then they don't have to worry about how that baby will grow. The US will "wet nurse" that kid forever. Of course, the parents also suck up the benefits all on the tax payers dime.

Once they taste the benefits of living here - they want it all. Now they demand these benefits even though they are illegal. The following is a list of prominent Latinos and what they have to say:

**

HISPANIC LEADERS SPEAK OUT!

<u>Augustin Cebada</u>, Brown Berets; "Go back to Boston! Go back to Plymouth Rock, Pilgrims! Get out! We are the future. You are old and tired. Go on. We have beaten you. Leave like beaten rats. You old white people. It is your duty to die . . Through love of having children, we are going to take over.

<u>Richard Alatorre</u>, Los Angeles City Council. "They're afraid we're going to take over the governmental institutions and other institutions. They're right. We will take them over . . . We are here to stay."

<u>Excelsior</u>, the national newspaper of Mexico, "The American Southwest seems to be slowly returning to the jurisdiction of Mexico without firing a single shot."

<u>Professor Jose Angel Gutierrez</u>, University of Texas; "We have an aging white America. They are not making babies. They are dying. The explosion is in our population . . . I love it. They are shitting in their pants with fear. I love it."

Art Torres, Chairman of the California Democratic Party, "Remember 187-- proposition to deny taxpayer funds for services to non-citizens--was the last gasp of white America in California."

Gloria Molina, Los Angeles County Supervisor, "We are politicizing every single one of these new citizens that are becoming citizens of this country . . . I gotta tell you that a lot of people are saying, "I'm going to go out there and vote because I want to pay them back."

Mario Obledo, California Coalition of Hispanic Organizations and California State Secretary of Health, Education and Welfare under Governor Jerry Brown, also awarded the Presidential Medal of Freedom by President Bill Clinton, "California is going to be a Hispanic state. Anyone who doesn't like it should leave."

Jose Pescador Osuna, Mexican Consul General, "We are practicing 'La Reconquista' in California."

<u>Professor Fernando Guerra</u>, Loyola Marymount University; "We need to avoid a white backlash by using codes understood by Latinos . . . "

Are these just the words of a few extremists? Consider that we could fill up many pages with such quotes. Also, consider that these are mainstream Mexican leaders.

THE U.S. VS MEXICO:
On February 15, 1998, the U.S. and Mexican soccer teams met at the Los Angeles Coliseum. The crowd was overwhelmingly pro-Mexican even though most lived in this country. They booed during the National Anthem and U.S. flags were held upside down. As the match progressed, supporters of the U.S. team were insulted, pelted with projectiles, punched and spat upon. Beer and trash were thrown at the U.S. players before and after the match. The coach of the U.S. team, Steve Sampson said, "This was the most painful experience I have ever had in this profession."

Did you know that immigrants from Mexico and other non-European countries can come to this country and get preferences in jobs, education, and government contracts? It's called affirmative action or racial privilege. The Emperor of Japan or the President of Mexico could migrate here and immediately be eligible for special rights unavailable for Americans of European descent. Recently, a vote was taken in the U.S. Congress to end this practice. It was defeated. Every single Democratic senator except Ernest Hollings voted to maintain special privileges for Hispanic, Asian and African immigrants. They were joined by thirteen Republicans. Bill Clinton and Al Gore have repeatedly stated that they believe that massive immigration from countries like Mexico is good. They have also backed special privileges for these immigrants.

Corporate America has signed on to the idea that minorities and third world immigrants should get special, privileged status.   Some examples are Exxon, Texaco, Merrill Lynch, Boeing, Paine Weber, Starbucks and many more.

DID YOU KNOW?:
Did you know that Mexico regularly intercedes on the side of the defense in criminal cases involving Mexican nationals?   Did you know that Mexico hasNEVER extradited a Mexican national accused of murder in the U.S. in spite of agreements to do so? According to the L.A. Times, Orange County, California is home to 275 gangs with 17,000 members; 98% of which are Mexican and Asian. How's your county doing?

According to a New York Times article dated May 19, 1994, 20 years after the great influx of legal immigrants from Southeast Asia, 30% are still on welfare compared to 8% of households nationwide. A Wall Street Journal editorial dated December 5, 1994 quotes law enforcement officials as stating that Asian mobsters are the "greatest criminal challenge the country faces." Not bad for a group that is still under 5% of the population.

Is education important to you? Here are the words of a teacher who spent over 20 years in the Los Angeles School system. "Imagine teachers in classes containing 30-40 students of widely varying attention spans and motivation, many of whom aren't fluent in English. Educators seek learning materials likely to reach the majority of students and that means fewer words and math problems and more pictures and multicultural references."

WHEN I WAS YOUNG:
When I was young, I remember hearing about the immigrants that came through Ellis Island. They wanted to learn English. They wanted to breath free. They wanted to become Americans. Now too many immigrants come here with demands. They demand to be taught in their own language. They demand special privileges--affirmative

action. They demand ethnic studies that glorify their culture.

****

We've been at war with Mexico several times in our history. When this country was young, Mexico played a huge role testing our resolve. The Texas Independence War in 1835 - 1836 started it all. The US - Mexican war from 1846 - 1848 continued the hostilities. We also had the Bear Flag Revolution in California.

It needs to be noted that Los Angeles, California is the second largest Mexican city outside of Mexico City. Now put that in your pipe and smoke it. There is no wonder that the LA City Council voted to ban their travel to Arizona due to Arizona's recent illegal immigration law. Of course now Arizona is threatening to cut off LA's power. It seems like LA just doesn't have enough things to worry about and they have to find things to piss people off.

Though many Mexicans that are citizens of the USA are also attached at the hip with their home country. Recently when Mexico played the US in soccer in LA their true feelings came out and were an embarrassment to all that watched - except the Mexicans.

The students also are embarrassing when they act like they are something special.

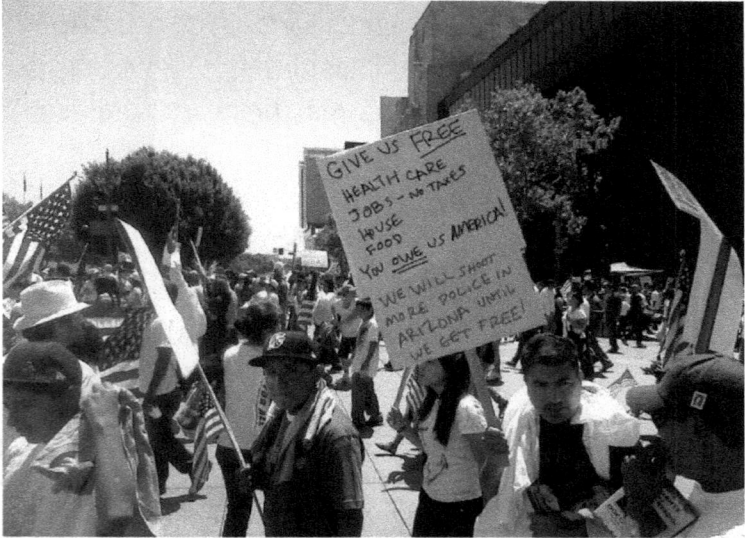

Who do they think they are?

This really represents their true feel-ings.

**

This is a very good summation of the reasoning behind the controversial AZ bill signed into law last week.. You certainly won't see this viewpoint in the press..

GFA

Subject: Arizona State Senator Sylvia Allen.

"I want to explain SB 1070"

I'm Arizona State Senator Sylvia Allen. I want to explain SB 1070 which I voted for and was just signed by Governor Jan Brewer.
Rancher Rob Krantz was murdered by the drug cartel on his ranch a month ago. I participated in a senate hearing two weeks ago on the border violence, here is just some of the highlights from those who testified.

The people who live within 60 to 80 miles of the Arizona/Mexico Border have for years been terrorized and have pleaded for help to stop the daily invasion of humans who cross their property . One Rancher testified that 300 to 1200 people a DAY come across his ranch vandalizing his property, stealing his vehicles and property, cutting down his fences, and leaving trash. In the last two years he has found 17 dead bodies and two Koran bibles.

Another rancher testified that daily drugs are brought across his ranch in a military operation. A point man with a machine gun goes in front, 1/2 mile behind are the guards fully armed, 1/2 mile behind them are the drugs, behind the drugs 1/2 mile are more guards. These people are violent and they will kill anyone who gets in the way. This was not the only rancher we heard that day that talked about the drug trains.

One man told of two illegal's who came upon his property one shot in the back and the other in the arm by the drug runners who had forced them to carry the drugs and then shot them. Daily they listen to gun fire during the night it is not safe to leave his family alone on the ranch and they can't leave the ranch for fear of nothing being left when they come back.

The border patrol is not on the border. They have set up 60 miles away with check points that do nothing to stop the invasion. They are not allowed to use force in stopping anyone who is entering. They run around chasing them, if they get their hands on them then they can take them back across the border.

Federal prisons have over 35% illegal's and 20% of Arizona prisons are filled with illegal's. In the last few years 80% of our law enforcement that have been killed or wounded have been by an illegal.

The majority of people coming now are people we need to be worried about. The ranchers told us that they have seen a change in the people coming they are not just those who are looking for work and a better life.

The Federal Government has refused for years to do anything to help the border states. We have been over run and once they are here we have the burden of funding state services that they use. Education cost have been over a billion dollars. The healthcare cost billions of dollars. Our State is broke, $3.5 billion deficit and we have many serious decisions to make. One is that we do not have the money to care for any who are not here legally. It has to stop.

The border can be secured. We have the technology we have the ability to stop this invasion. We must know who is coming and they must come in an organized manner legally so that we can assimilate them into our population and protect the sovereignty of our country. We are a nation of laws. We have a responsibility to protect our citizens and to protect the integrity of our country and the government which we live under.

I would give amnesty today to many, but here is the problem, we dare not do this until the Border is secure. It will do no good to forgive them because thousands will come behind them and we will be over run to the point that there will no longer be the United States of America but a North American Union of open borders. I ask you what form of government will we live under? How long will it be before we will be just like Mexico, Canada or any of the other Central American or South American countries? We have already lost our language, everything must be printed in Spanish also. We have already lost our history it is no longer taught in our schools. And we have lost our borders.

The leftist media has distorted what SB 1070 will do. It is not going to set up a Nazi Germany. Are you kidding. The ACLU and the leftist courts will do everything to protect those who are here illegally, but it was an effort to try and stop illegal's from setting up businesses, and employment, and receiving state services and give the ability to local law enforcement when there is probable cause like a traffic stop to determine if they are here legally. Federal law is very clear if you are here on a visa you must have your papers on you at all times. That is the law. In Arizona all you need to show you are a legal citizen is a driver license, MVD identification card, Native American Card, or a Military ID. This is what you need to vote, get a hunting license, etc.. So nothing new has been added to this law. No one is going to be stopped walking down the street etc... The Socialist who are in power in DC are angry because we dare try and do something and that something the Socialist wants us to do is just let them come. They want the "Transformation" to continue.

Maybe it is too late to save America. Maybe we are not worthy of freedom anymore. But as an elected official I must try to do what I can to protect our Constitutional Republic. Living in America is not a right just because you can walk across the border. Being an American is a responsibility and it comes by respecting and upholding the Constitution the law of our land which says what you must do to be a citizen of this country. Freedom is not free.

****

**

It may be talking about California , but this is happening all across America .

Cheap Tomatoes

THIS HAS GOT TO BE PASSED ALONG TO AS MANY AS POSSIBLE OR WE WILL ALL GO DOWN THE DRAIN BECAUSE A FEW DON'T CARE.

This English teacher has phrased it the best I've seen yet.
This should make everyone think, be you Democrat, Republican or Independent

From a California school teacher - - -
"As you listen to the news about the student protests over illegal immigration, there are some things that you should be aware of:

I am in charge of the English-as-a-second-language department at a large southern California high school which is designated a Title 1 school, meaning that its students average lower socio-economic and income levels

Most of the schools you are hearing about, South Gate High, Bell Gardens , Huntington Park , etc., where these students are protesting, are also Title 1 schools.

Title 1 schools are on the free breakfast and free lunch program. When I say free breakfast, I'm not talking a glass of milk and roll -- but a full breakfast and cereal bar with fruits and juices that would make a Marriott proud. The waste of this food is monumental, with trays and trays of it being dumped in the trash uneaten.

I estimate that well over 50% of these students are obese or at least moderately overweight. About 75% or more DO have cell phones. The school also provides day care centers for the unwed teenage pregnant girls (some as young as 13) so they can attend class without the inconvenience of having to arrange for babysitters or having family watch their kids.

I was ordered to spend $700,000 on my department or risk losing funding for the upcoming year even though there was little need for anything; my budget was already substantial. I ended up buying new computers for the computer learning center, half of which, one month later, have been carved with graffiti by the appreciative students who obviously feel humbled and grateful to have a free education in America.

I have had to intervene several times for young and substitute teachers whose classes consist of many illegal immigrant students, here in the country less then 3 months, who raised so much hell with the female teachers, calling them "Putas"(whores) and throwing things, that the teachers were in tears.

Free medical, free education, free food, free day care etc., etc, etc. Is it any wonder they feel entitled to not only be in this country but to demand rights, privileges and entitlements?

To those who want to point out how much these illegal immigrants contribute to our society because they LIKE their gardener and housekeeper and they like to pay less for tomatoes: spend some time in the real world of illegal immigration and see the TRUE costs.

Higher insurance, medical facilities closing, higher medical costs, more crime, lower standards of education in our schools, overcrowding, new diseases. For me, I'll pay more for tomatoes.

Americans, We need to wake up.

It does, however, have everything to do with culture: It involves an American third-world culture that does not value education, that accepts children getting pregnant and dropping out of school by 15 and that refuses to assimilate, and an American culture that has become so weak and worried about "political correctness" that we don't have the will to do anything about it.

If this makes your blood boil, as it did mine, forward this to everyone you know.

CHEAP LABOR? Isn't that what the whole immigration issue is about?

Business doesn't want to pay a decent wage.

Consumers don't want expensive produce.

Government will tell you Americans don't want the jobs.

But the bottom line is cheap labor. The phrase "cheap labor" is a myth, a farce, and a lie. There is no such thing as "cheap labor."

Take, for example, an illegal alien with a wife and five children. He takes a job for $5.00 or 6.00/hour. At that wage, with six dependents, he pays no income tax, yet at the end of the year, if he files an Income Tax Return, he gets an "earned income credit" of up to $3,200 free.

He qualifies for Section 8 housing and subsidized rent.

He qualifies for food stamps.

He qualifies for free (no deductible, no co-pay) health care.

His children get free breakfasts and lunches at school.

He requires bilingual teachers and books.

He qualifies for relief from high energy bills.

If they are, or become, aged, blind or disabled, they qualify for SSI. If qualified for SSI they can qualify for Medicare.
All of this is at (OUR) taxpayer's expense.

He doesn't worry about car insurance, life insurance, or homeowners insurance.

Taxpayers provide Spanish language signs, bulletins and printed material.

He and his family receive the equivalent of $20.00 to $30.00/hour in benefits.

Working Americans are lucky to have $5.00 or $6..00/hour left after paying their bills AND his.

Cheap labor? YEAH RIGHT!
THESE ARE THE QUESTIONS WE SHOULD BE ADDRESSING TO THE CONGRESSIONAL MEMBERS OF EITHER PARTY. 'AND WHEN

THEY LIE TO US AND DON'T DO AS THEY SAY, WE SHOULD REPLACE THEM .

****

**

MEXICO IS ANGRY !

Three cheers for Arizona

The shoe is on the other foot and the Mexicans from the State of Sonora, Mexico dont like it.
Can you believe the nerve of these people? It's almost funny.
The State of Sonora is angry at the influx of Mexicans into Mexico . Nine state legislators from the Mexican State of Sonora traveled to Tucson to complain about Arizona 's new employer crackdown on illegals from Mexico .
It seems that many Mexican illegals are returning to their hometowns and the officials in the Sonora state government are ticked off.

A delegation of nine state legislators from Sonora was in Tucson on Tuesday to state that Arizona 's new Employer Sanctions Law will have a devastating effect on the Mexican state.

At a news conference, the legislators said that Sonora, - Arizona's southern neighbor, - made up of mostly small towns, - cannot handle the demand for housing, jobs and schools that it will face as Mexican workers return to their hometowns from the USA without jobs or money.

The Arizona law, which took effect Jan. 1, punishes Arizona employers who knowingly hire individuals without valid legal documents to work in the United States .

Penalties include suspension of, or loss of, their business license.

The Mexican legislators are angry because their own citizens are returning to their hometowns, placing a burden on THEIR state government. 'How can Arizona pass a law like this?' asked Mexican

Rep Leticia Amparano-Gamez, who represents Nogales .

'There is not one person living in Sonora who does not have a friend or relative working in Arizona ,' she said, speaking in Spanish. 'Mexico is not prepared for this, for the tremendous problems it will face as more and more Mexicans working in Arizona and who were sending money to their families return to their hometowns in Sonora without jobs,' she said. 'We are one family, socially and economically,' she said of the people of Sonora and Arizona .

****

Here are some simple rules to make this problem go away. Thousands and thousands of immigrants had to follow these same rules before they were able to enjoy the fruits of the "freedom tree". Yes, hard work was involved, but the people did it without much complaining. You have to realize that over 95% of those crossing the border did not come to mow my lawn or pick my tomatoes.

**

Map of My Country

Let me make this perfectly clear!

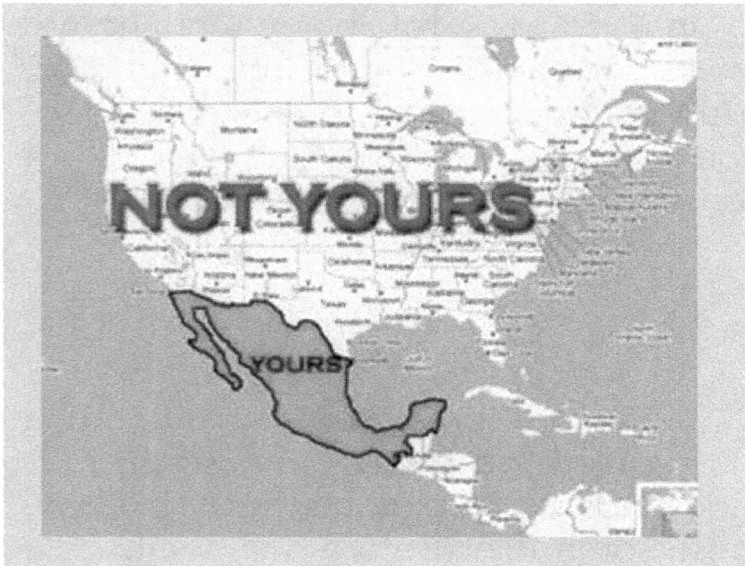

THIS IS MY COUNTRY!

And, because I make This statement DOES NOT Mean I'm against immigration!!!

Ron Berger   140

YOU ARE WELCOME HERE, IN MY COUN-
TRY!

Welcome! To come through legally:

1. Get a sponsor!

2. Get a place to lay your head!

3. Get a job!

4. Live By OUR Rules!

5. Pay YOUR Taxes!

And

6. Learn the LANGUAGE like immigrants

have in the past!!!

AND

7. Please don't demand that we hand
over our lifetime savings of Social Security Funds to you.

Ron Berger   141

If you don't want to forward this for fear of offending someone,

Then YOU'RE PART OF THE PROBLEM!

When will AMERICANS STOP giving away THEIR RIGHTS???

We've gone so far the other way... bent over backwards not to offend anyone.

But it seems no one cares about the AMERICAN CITIZEN that's being offended!

WAKE UP America !!!

****

Here is a little newspaper article from Victoria, Texas after the local Hispanic leaders called for a boycott to voice their displeasure to pending immigration legislation. The impact was far different than they had hoped for.

**

Victoria, Texas is a town about 80 miles west of Houston. Local Hispanic leaders there, in opposition to pending Immigration Legislation, boycotted all Caucasian owned businesses last month as a demonstration of their economic impact on the community. The boycott was declared a success by the Hispanic community, noting revenue in Caucasian owned businesses was down by 19 percent. Business owners declared the boycott a success as well, pointing out that shoplifting was reduced by 77 percent, money orders sent out of the country were down by 97 percent, and the cost of daily clean-up and trash collection was down by 84 percent. Shoppers reported they could actually hear English being spoken throughout the community for the first time in recent memory, and customers paid for purchases with real money, not government debit cards or food stamps!

****

There is an upside to all this commotion and this article shows us a good example. Many Mexicans are not used to "clean living" and they bring that trait with them when they cross the border.

We can't drink their water, but they can. They have built up a tolerance for their kind of living that can be readily seen just by looking at their places they call home. Of course they may have three or four families living in their "home" which accounts for all those run down vehicles parked all over the lawns.

Obviously not all Mexicans came here to be gardeners or landscapers. Their claim to fame lies somewhere else, like having babies born in the USA. It's not unusual to see a mother walking down the street with two or three in tow, pushing a carriage and being four or five months pregnant. You can't send Mom & Dad back to Mexico and leave "citizens of the USA" here to fend for themselves. Of course I'm sure the government would figure out a plan to solve that. Surely permanent care facilities could be arranged which would resemble Germanys in the hay days of the 3rd Reich.

This is what Speaker Nancy Pelosi has to say about immigration:

**

Pelosi Calls for Amnesty for Illegal Aliens
Thursday, May 13, 2010
By Nicholas Ballasy, Video Reporter

(CNSNews.com) -- Speaking at the Asian-American and Pacific Islanders Summit held at the Capitol on Wednesday, House Speaker Nancy Pelosi called for amnesty for illegal aliens in the United States, a proposal she called a "path to legalization."

"Hopefully, we will be moving toward comprehensive immigration reform that secures our borders, enforces our laws, protects our workers, honors family unification and has a path to legalization--so that we have certainty in our country and respect for the contributions that newcomers bring to us," she said on Capitol Hill on Wednesday.

House Minority Leader John Boehner's (R-Ohio) office told CNSNews.com that Boehner "disagrees" with Pelosi's comments and thinks immigration reform will not pass this year.

"Mr. Boehner has said that no one believes we will do immigration reform this year," said Michael Steel, Boehner's press secretary. "Democrats are only talking about it to gin up their political base."

Speaker Pelosi also spoke about immigration reform last week on Capitol Hill at the Catholic Community Conference. At that event, she said she had asked Catholic bishops to speak from the pulpit about how immigration reform was a "manifestation of our living the Gospels."

"I would hope that there's one thing that we can do working together as we go forward that speaks to what the Bible tells us about the dignity and worth of every person, and that is on the subject of immigration," she said. "Because I think the church is going to have to play a very major role in how we, in how people are treated."

"The cardinals, the archbishops, the bishops that come to me and say, 'We want you to pass immigration reform,' and I say, 'But I want you to speak about it from the pulpit,'" said Pelosi. "I want you to instruct your, whatever the communication is -- the people, some of them, oppose immigration reform are sitting in those pews and you have to tell them that this is a manifestation of our living the Gospels."

"Our patron saint of San Francisco, St. Francis of Assisi, he said, 'preach the gospel --sometimes use words,'" said Pelosi. "We need the words to be said because it isn't being picked up automatically."

Speaker Pelosi voted against the "Secure Fence Act of 2006," which funded the construction a 700-mile-long double-reinforced fence along the Mexican border. President George W. Bush signed the legislation into law in October 2006. Pelosi has favored amnesty for illegal aliens in the past but has not brought a bill that would provide amnesty to a vote in the House since she became speaker after the 2006 election. In 2004, when she was given the "Legislative Award" of the League of United Latin American Citizens, she said: "We do not need a temporary worker program; we need a meaningful pathway to citizenship."

House Speaker Nancy Pelosi's office did not respond to CNSNews.com's inquiries about her statement Wednesday at Asian-American and Pacific Islanders Summit.

****

The only thing she is looking at are the "new votes" for the liberal side of the House floor. She does not understand that those new votes cost the tax payer millions of dollars a year just to have them vote. I feel that the time to repeal

Nancy is this year - (2010). She needs to retire - at great cost to the tax payer I might add - but then again it will be so much cheaper to kick her out now then to have her in Washington for another two years. We just can't afford her or her like minded idiots to run this country in the ground.

Recently, BO ordered 1200 National Guard troops to the US/Mexican border to help guard our southern border. It doesn't take a mathematical genius to figure out that 1200 troops equals about one soldier every two miles or so. Of course there would be officers in that group so it could be one for every three miles or so very easily. That's really going to help BO. Senator McCain has called for 6,000 troops to man the border.

I'm sure BO thinks that 1200 troops will appease those that believe the border should be sealed off tight. He just doesn't understand that even though he said he went to Columbia, Yale, etc, etc, - or where ever - the normal American is definitely better at math than he is.

Activists blast Mexico's immigration law
Hector Vazquez, 36, of Honduras talks about his experiences as an undocumented migrant at his temporary camp earlier this month in Tultitlan, Mexico.

By Chris Hawley, USA TODAY
TULTITLN, Mexico — Arizona's new law forcing local police to take a greater role in enforcing immigration law has caused a lot of criticism from Mexico, the largest single source of illegal immigrants in the United States.
But in Mexico, illegal immigrants receive terrible treatment from corrupt Mexican authorities, say people involved in the system.
And Mexico has a law that is no different from Arizona's that empowers local police to check the immigration documents of people suspected of not being in the country legally.
"There (in the United States), they'll deport you," Hector Vázquez, an illegal immigrant from Honduras, said as he rested in a makeshift camp with other migrants under a highway bridge in Tultitlán. "In

Mexico they'll probably let you go, but they'll beat you up and steal everything you've got first."
Mexican authorities have harshly criticized Arizona's SB1070, a law that requires local police to check the status of persons suspected of being illegal immigrants. The law provides that a check be done in connection with another law enforcement event, such as a traffic stop, and also permits Arizona citizens to file lawsuits against local authorities for not fully enforcing immigration laws.

Mexico's Foreign Ministry said the law "violates inalienable human rights" and Democrats in Congress applauded Mexican President Felipe Calderón's criticisms of the law in a speech he gave on Capitol Hill last week.
Yet Mexico's Arizona-style law requires local police to check IDs. And Mexican police freely engage in racial profiling and routinely harass Central American migrants, say immigration activists.
"The Mexican government should probably clean up its own house before

looking at someone else's," said Melissa Vertíz, spokeswoman for the Fray Matías de Córdova Human Rights Center in Tapachula, Mexico.

In one six-month period from September 2008 through February 2009, at least 9,758 migrants were kidnapped and held for ransom in Mexico — 91 of them with the direct participation of Mexican police, a report by the National Human Rights Commission said. Other migrants are routinely stopped and shaken down for bribes, it said.

A separate survey conducted during one month in 2008 at 10 migrant shelters showed Mexican authorities were behind migrant attacks in 35 of 240 cases, or 15%.

Most migrants in Mexico are Central Americans who are simply passing through on their way to the United States, human rights groups say. Others are Guatemalans who live and work along Mexico's southern border, mainly as farm workers, as maids, or in bars and restaurants.

The Central American migrants headed to the United States travel mainly on freight trains, stopping to rest and beg for food at rail crossings like the one in Tultitlán, an industrial suburb of Mexico City.

On a recent afternoon, Victor Manuel Beltrán Rodríguez of Managua, Nicaragua, trudged between the cars at a stop light, his hand outstretched. "Can you give me a peso? I'm from Nicaragua," he said. Every 10 cars or so, a motorist would roll down the window and hand him a few coins. In a half-hour he had collected 10 pesos, about 80 U.S. cents, enough for a taco.

Beltrán Rodríguez had arrived in Mexico with 950 pesos, about $76, enough to last him to the U.S. border. But near Tierra Blanca, Veracruz, he says municipal police had detained him, driven him to a deserted road and taken his money. He had been surviving since then by begging.

Abuses by Mexican authorities have persisted even as Mexico has relaxed its rules against illegal immigrants in recent years, according to the National Human Rights Commission.

In 2008, Mexico softened the punishment for illegal immigrants, from a maximum 10 years in prison to a maximum fine of $461. Most detainees are taken to detention centers and put on buses for home.

Mexican law calls for six to 12 years of prison and up to $46,000 in fines for anyone who shelters or transports illegal immigrants. The Supreme Court ruled in 2008 that the law applies only to people who do it for money.

For years, the Mexican government has allowed charity groups to openly operate migrant shelters, where travelers can rest for a few days on their journey north. The government also has a special unit of immigration agents, known as Grupo Beta, who patrol the countryside in orange pickups, helping immigrants who are in trouble.

At the same time, Article 67 of Mexico's immigration law requires that all authorities "whether federal, local or municipal" demand to see visas if approached by a foreigner and to hand over migrants to immigration authorities.

"In effect, this means that migrants who suffer crimes, including kidnapping, prefer not to report them to avoid ... being detained by immigration authorities and returned to their country," the National Human Rights Commission said in a report last year.

As a result, the clause has strengthened gangs who abuse migrants, rights activists say.

"That Article 67 is an obstacle that urgently has to be removed," said Alberto Herrera, executive director of Amnesty International Mexico. "It has worsened this vicious cycle of abuse and impunity, and the same thing could happen (in Arizona)."

A bill passed by the Mexican Senate on Oct. 6 would eliminate the ID requirement in Article 67 and replace it with language saying "No attention in matters of human rights or the provision of justice shall be denied or restricted on any level (of government) to foreigners who require it, regardless of their migration status."

The Mexican House of Representatives approved a similar measure on March 16, but added a clause requiring the government to set aside funds to take care of foreigners during times of disaster. The revised bill has been stuck in the Senate's Population and Development Committee since then.

To discourage migrants from speaking out about abuse, Mexican authorities often tell detainees they will have to stay longer in detention centers if they file a complaint, Vertíz said.

A March 2007 order allows Mexican immigration agents to give "humanitarian visas" to migrants who have suffered crimes in Mexico. But the amnesty is not automatic, and most migrants don't know to ask for it, the commission said.

Hawley is Latin America correspondent for USA TODAY and The Arizona Republic

****

Here is an example of the type of laws we need to enact:

**

Should we all boycott Mexico??????

New Immigration Laws:

1 There will be no special bilingual programs in the schools.
* *

2. All ballots will be in this nation's language.
* *

3. All government business will be conducted in our language.
* *

4. Non-residents will NOT have the right to vote no matter how long they are here.
* *

5. Non-citizens will NEVER be able to hold political office
* *

6 Foreigners will not be a burden to the taxpayers. No welfare, no food stamps,

no health care, or other government assistance programs. Any burden will be deported.

* *

7. Foreigners can invest in this country, but it must be an amount at least equal to 40,000 times the daily minimum wage.

* *

8. If foreigners come here and buy land... options will be restricted. Certain parcels including waterfront property are reserved for citizens naturally born into this country.

* *

9.. Foreigners may have no protests; no demonstrations, no waving of a foreign flag, no political organizing, no bad-mouthing our president or his policies. These will lead to deportation.

* *

10. If you do come to this country illegally, you will be actively hunted &, when caught, sent to jail until your deportation can be arranged. All assets will be taken from you.

* *

Too strict?......

The above laws are the current immigration laws of MEXICO !!!

****

That will soon be our only immigration law.

Ron Berger   160

When Mexico's President was in the USA In May, 2010 he made a lot of derogatory statements about Arizona's new law. Either he is totally stupid or he hans't a clue what Mexico's laws are. The worst thing that happened was that BO agreed with him and chimed in to criticize Arizona. Now you have two "heads of state" that are really stupid and haven't a clue what's going on. <u>The only way to get rid of stupidity is to vote it out.</u>

**

Mexican President Denounces Arizona Law Despite Laws Against Illegal Immigration in His Own Country
Thursday, May 20, 2010
By Penny Starr, Senior Staff Writer

At a May 19, 2010 press conference in the White House Rose Garden, President Barack Obama and Mexican President Felipe Calderon both criticized the new

illegal immigration law in Arizona. (CNSNews.com/Penny Starr)
(Update: Adds Mexican President Calderon's comments to CNN's Wolf Blitzer about Mexico's revised immigration law.)

(CNSNews.com) – At a joint press conference in the White House Rose Garden on Wednesday, President Barack Obama and Mexican President Felipe Calderon criticized Arizona's new law against illegal immigration.

Calderon, through a translator, called the law "discriminatory," while Obama said the wording of the law was "troublesome" and could lead to innocent people being "harassed or arrested."

"I think the Arizona law has the potential of being applied in a discriminatory fashion," Obama said. He said a "fair reading of the language of the statute" raises the possibility that individuals suspected of being in the country illegally could be "harassed or arrested."

Calderon said while he remains "respectful of the internal policies of the United States," he firmly rejects criminalizing "migration" so that "people who work and provide things for this nation (USA) will be treated as criminals."

In Calderon's Mexico, however, illegal immigration is punished with fines and deportations.

President Obama -- who took only two questions from foreign journalists at the press conference -- said he has asked the Justice Department to examine the Arizona immigration law for possible civil rights violations. (CNSNews.com/Penny Starr)

"I know that we share the interest in promoting dignified, legal and orderly living conditions to all migrant workers," Calderon said through a translator in his prepared remarks. "Many of them, despite their significant contribution to the economy and to the society of the United States, still live in the shadows, and occasionally, as in Arizona, they even face discrimination."

Obama -- who only took two questions, both from foreign journalists -- said he has asked the Justice Department to look into the Arizona law. Last week, Attorney General Eric Holder told the House Judiciary Committee he had not read the law that Obama and members of his administration have denounced since it was signed by Arizona governor Jan Brewer on April 23.

The two leaders' criticism comes despite revisions to the Arizona law that expressly prohibit police from racial profiling.

The revised Arizona law specifically states that a person's immigration status can be checked only if an individual is stopped for some other, valid reason. "A lawful stop, detention or arrest must be in the enforcement of any other law or ordinance of a county, city or town or this state," the revised law says.

Mexican President Felipe Calderon has not only criticized the Arizona law but has threatened to boycott Arizona. The immigration laws in Mexico, however, are stricter in some ways than U.S. immigration laws. (CNSNews.com/Penny Starr)

By contrast, Mexican immigration law, revised in 2009, gives Mexican officials the right to check people's immigration status, and if someone is found to be in the country illegally, they can be fined and deported. The law also requires foreigners to register with the government.

'We send them back'

Wednesday afternoon, after appearing at the White House with President Obama, Calderon appeared on CNN's "The Situation Room" with Wolf Blitzer, where he made the point that illegal immigration is no longer a crime in Mexico, under the 2009 revisions.

"So if people want to come from Guatemala or Honduras or El Salvador or

Nicaragua, they want to just come into Mexico, they can just walk in?," Blitzer asked.

"No," Calderon said. They need to fill out a form and undergo a criminal background check, he said.

"Do Mexican police go around asking for papers of people they suspect are illegal immigrants?" Blitzer asked.

"Of course. Of course, in the border, we are asking the people, who are you?" Calderon replied.

Once foreigners are legally admitted to the country, "what the Mexican police do is, of course, enforce the law," Calderon said.

Can people who sneak into Mexico from Central America, for example, get a job? Blitzer asked.

No, no, Calderon replied. "If – if some-body do that without permission, we send back -- we send back them."

"You find them and you send them back?" Blitzer asked.

"Yes," Calderon confirmed. He admitted that Americans have a "very power-ful argument" when they say that Arizona and other border states are only trying to do what Mexico itself does with illegal immigrants – find them and send them back.

'Mexicans interfering'

Rep. Lamar Smith (R-Texas), the ranking member on the House Judiciary Committee, sent a letter to Secretary of State Hillary Clinton -- who hosted Calderon for lunch at the State Department following the Rose Garden press conference – objecting to Calderon pressuring the U.S. about its immigration laws and policies.

"In their advocacy efforts on behalf of Mexican citizens living in the United States, President Calderon and other officials of the Mexican government have crossed the line and are interfering in the internal affairs of the United States," Smith said in a statement on Wednesday.

"It is well recognized in international law that immigration controls are an internal matter, and not subject to international scrutiny," Smith said. "Yet, President Calderon has opposed the recently enacted Arizona immigration law, which in fact mirrors federal law.

"Mexican government officials openly talk of a Mexican government boycott of Arizona, but make no effort to prevent their citizens from going there," Smith said. "American public officials have the right and the responsibility to implement an immigration policy that is in the best interests of the American people."

****

THOSE PEOPLE *in* ARIZONA ARE TRYING TO MAKE ILLEGAL ALIENS .... GASP! ...

ILLEGAL!

FULLER

A short message to BO:

**

Dear President Obama:

I'm planning to move my family and extended family into Mexico for my health, and I would like to ask you to assist me.

We're planning to simply walk across the border from the U.S. into Mexico, and

Ron Berger   170

we'll need your help to make a few arrangements.

We plan to skip all the legal stuff like visas, passports, immigration quotas and laws.

I'm sure they handle those things the same way you do here. So, would you mind telling your buddy, President Calderon, that I'm on my way over?

Please let him know that I will be expecting the following:

1. Free medical care for my entire family.

2. English-speaking government bureaucrats for all services I might need, whether I use them or not.

3. Please print all Mexican government forms in English.

4. I want my grandkids to be taught Spanish by English-speaking (bi-lingual) teachers.

5. Tell their schools they need to include classes on American culture and history..

6. I want my grandkids to see the American flag on one of the flag poles at their school.

7. Please plan to feed my grandkids at school for both breakfast and lunch.

8. I will need a local Mexican driver's license so I can get easy access to government services.

9. I do plan to get a car and drive in Mexico but I don't plan to purchase car insurance, and I probably won't make any special effort to learn local traffic laws.

10. In case one of the Mexican police officers does not get the memo from

their   president to leave me alone, please be sure that every patrol car has at least one English-speaking officer.

11. I plan to fly the   U.S. flag from my house top, put U. S. flag decals on my car, and have a gigantic celebration on July 4th. I do not want any complaints or negative comments from the locals.

12. I would also like to have a nice job without paying any taxes, or have any labor or tax laws enforced on any business I may start.

13. Please have the president tell all the Mexican people to be extremely nice and never say critical things about me or my family, or about the strain we might place on their economy.

14. I want to receive free food stamps.

15. Naturally, I'll expect free rent subsidies.

16. I'll need Income tax credits so although I don't pay Mexican Taxes, I'll receive money from the government.

17. Please arrange it so that the Mexican Gov't pays $4,500 to help me buy a new car.

18. Oh yes, I almost forgot, please enroll me free into the Mexican Social Security program so that I'll get a monthly income in retirement. I know this is an easy request because you already do all these things for all his people who walk over to the U.S. from Mexico. I am sure that President Calderon won't mind returning the favor if you ask him nicely.

Thank you so much for your kind help. You're the man BRO!!!

****

Our country is starting to get the message. This is what Oklahoma is doing and a number of others are planning similar methods:

**

OKLAHOMA MAY JUST BE THE PLACE TO LIVE!

An update from Oklahoma :

Oklahoma law passed, 37 to 9, had a few liberals in the mix, an amendment to place the Ten Commandments on the front entrance to the state capitol. The feds in D.C., along with the ACLU, said it would be a mistake. Hey this is a conservative state, based on Christian values...! HB 1330

Guess what......... Oklahoma did it anyway.

Oklahoma recently passed a law in the state to incarcerate all illegal immigrants, and ship them back to where they came from unless they want to get a green card and become an American citizen. They all scattered. HB 1804. Hope we didn't send any of them to your state. This was against the advice of the Federal Government, and the ACLU, they said it would be a mistake.

Guess what......... Oklahoma did it anyway.

Recently we passed a law to include DNA samples from any and all illegals to the Oklahoma database, for criminal investigative purposes. Pelosi said it was unconstitutional. SB 1102

Guess what....... Oklahoma did it anyway.

Several weeks ago, we passed a law, declaring Oklahoma as a Sovereign state, not under the Federal Government directives. Joining Texas, Montana and Utah as the only states to do so. More states are likely to follow: Louisiana, Alabama, Georgia, the Carolina's, Tennessee, Kentucky, Missouri, Arkansas, West Virginia, Mississippi, Florida. Save your confederate money, it appears the South is about to rise up once again. HJR 1003

The federal Government has made bold steps to take away our guns. Oklahoma, a week ago, passed a law confirming people in this state have the right to bear arms and transport them in their vehicles. I'm sure that was a set back for the criminals (and Obamaites). Liberals didn't like it -- But ......

Guess what........... Oklahoma did it anyway.

Just this month, the state has voted and passed a law that ALL driver's license exams will be printed in English, and only English, and no other language. They have been called racist for doing this, but the fact is that ALL of the road signs are in English only. If you want to drive in Oklahoma , you must read and write English. Really simple.

By the way, Obama does not like any of this.

Guess what....who cares... Oklahoma is doing it anyway.

****

I leave this section with something to ponder:

**

Spelling -
Did you know that the words "race car" spelled backwards still spells "race car"?
That "eat" is the only word that, if you take the 1st letter and move it to the last, spells its past tense, ate"?

And if you rearrange the letters in "illegal immigrants," and add just a few more letters, it spells: "Go home you free-loading, benefit-grabbing, resource-sucking, baby-making, violent, non-English-speaking a**holes, and take those other hairy-faced, sandal-wearing, bomb-making, Camel-riding, goat-loving, raggedy-a** bastards with you?

How weird is that?

****

The US Government

BO, Congress and all the minions

The enemy from within

"It's all good folks -- Trust Us!"

How can this be? Our own government on my enemies list? Aren't the smiles on Pelosi and Ried's face comforting? Actually I'm sure they are quite sickening. I truly believe that they're more of a smirk than a smile.

Before BO gets his dues, I have to speak a little about his wife. There just seems to be something about that whole family that requires that we give them more than the job demands. I'm sure that by the time they leave the White House we will have given them more than enough to satisfy all the claims from all the other Blacks that believe America owes them something. Now take a look at this:

**

First Lady Michelle Obama's Servant List and Pay Scale

First Lady Requires More Than Twenty Attendants

1. $172,2000 - Sher, Susan (Chief Of Staff)

2. $140,000 - Frye, Jocelyn C . (Deputy Assistant to the President and Director of Policy And Projects For The First Lady)

3. $113,000 - Rogers, Desiree G (Special Assistant to the President and White House Social Secretary)

4. $102,000 - Johnston, Camille Y. (Special Assistant to the President and Director of Communications for the First Lady)

5. $100,000 - Winter, Melissa E. (Special Assistant to the President and Deputy Chief Of Staff to the First Lady)

6. $90,000 - Medina , David S. (Deputy Chief Of Staff to the First Lady)

7. $84,000 - Lelyveld, Catherine M. (Director and Press Secretary to the First Lady)

8. $75,000 - Starkey, Frances M. (Director of Scheduling and Advance for the First Lady)

9. $70,000 - Sanders, Trooper (Deputy Director of Policy and Projects for the First Lady)

10.. $65,000 - Burnough, Erinn J. (Deputy Director and Deputy Social Secretary)

11. $64,000 - Reinstein, Joseph B. (Deputy Director and Deputy Social Secretary)

12. $62,000 - Goodman, Jennifer R. (Deputy Director of Scheduling and Events Coordinator For The First Lady)

13. $60,000 - Fitts, Alan O. (Deputy Dir ector of Advance and Trip Director for the First Lady)

14. $57,500 - Lewis, Dana M. (Special Assistant and Personal Aide to the First Lady)

15.. $52,500 - Mustaphi, Semonti M. (Associate Director and Deputy Press Secretary To The First Lady)

16. $50,000 - Jarvis, Kristen E. (Special=2 0Assistant for Scheduling and Traveling Aide To The First Lady)

17. $45,000 - Lechtenberg, Tyler A. (Associate Director of Correspondence For The First Lady)

18. $43,000 - Tubman, Samantha (Deputy Associate Director, Social Office)

19. $40,000 - Boswell, Joseph J. (Executive Assistant to the Chief Of Staff to the First Lady)

20. $36,000 - Armbruster, Sally M. (Staff Assistant to the Social Secretary)

21. $35,000 - Bookey, Natalie (Staff Assistant)

22. $35,000 - Jackson, Deilia A. (Deputy Associate Director of Correspondence for the First Lady)

(This is community organizing at it's finest.)

There has NEVER been anyone in the White House at any time who has created such an army of staffers whose sole duties are the facilitation of the First Lady's social life. One wonders why she needs so much help, at taxpayer expense, when even Hillary, only had three; Jackie Kennedy one; Laura Bush one; and prior to Mamie Eisenhower social help came from the President's own pocket.

Note: This does not include makeup artist Ingrid Grimes-Miles, 49, and "First Hairstylist" Johnny Wright, 31, both of whom traveled aboard Air Force One to Europe.

FRIENDS.....THESE SALARIES ADD UP TO SIX MILLION, THREE HUNDRED SIXTY FOUR THOUSAND DOLLARS ($6,364,000)FOR THE 4 YEARS OF OFFICE????? AND WE ARE IN A RECESSION????? WELL....MOST OF US ARE. I GUESS IT'S OK TO SPEND WILDLY WHEN IT'S NOT YOUR OWN MONEY?????

Copyright 2009 Canada FreePress.Com

canadafreepress.com/i   ; ndex.php/article/12652

Yes, I know, The Canadian Free Press has to publish this because the USA media is too scared they might be considered racist. Sorry USA !

****

Now we can get down to King BO himself. In my last book I brought up the extravagant travel that he requires. I know that the President needs to be protected, but he should definitely pay the expenses when they are for political gain. The trip I talked about was to LA for the benefit of Senator Barbara Boxer. Several weeks later he also flew to San Francisco for another fund raiser for her. He really thinks his appearance is going to make a difference. Here is another King BO trip, but this time he is compared to the Queen of England.

I hope you get the drift. BO is extremely afraid that something will get into his soup or some bug is going to give him the shits or he might not give off the right impression. After all he is the "leader of the free world". I'm sure that is a title he firmly believes in.

**

COMMENTARY

An entourage surpassing the queen's

President Obama showed up at the G-20 summit in London with everything but the proverbial kitchen sink — although he did bring the White House chef and the kitchen staff.

DALE MCFEATTERS

Dale McFeatters writes for Scripps Howard News Service.

The heads of government in London for the G-20 summit are discussing serious and weighty issues, which in time will be duly reported on, but right now the British press is entranced by the sheer size of President Obama's traveling entourage. And no wonder.

Obama arrived with 500 staff in tow, including 200 Secret Service agents, a team of six doctors, the White House chef and kitchen staff with the president's own food and water.

And, according to the Evening Standard, he also came with "35 vehicles in all, four speech writers and 12 teleprompters." For sure, our president is not going to be at a loss for words.

The press duly reported on Air Force One and all its bells and whistles but also on the presence of the presidential helicopter, Marine One, and a fleet of identical decoys to ferry him from Stansted airport to central London.

Among all those vehicles is the presidential limousine, which one local paper mistakenly called Cadillac One, but is universally referred to as the Beast. The limo, reinforced with ceramic and titanium armor, carries tear gas cannon, night-vision devices and its own oxygen and is resistant to chemical and radiation attack. It is, marveled one reporter, a sort of mobile panic room. The Guardian called it "the ultimate in heavily armored transport."

The president is entitled to all the security, communications and support he feels necessary to do his job but surely, when we're trying to project a more restrained, humble image to the world, the president's huge retinue could be scaled back to something less than the triumphal march from "Aida."

****

But you have already read about this in your local newspaper ... oh no, you didn't? OK then, you saw it on CNN... no?... oh well.

Can you believe the arrogance of this President? Maybe he is asking them to kiss his feet.

BO is so busy being King that he cannot keep his eye on all the facets of government. He has hired a number of helpers, called Czars, to help him run this complicated country. Following is a list of Czars and what they do. Mindful - these were hired directly by BO and didn't require any confirmation by the Senate:

**

The Czars--Who are they and what do they do? Probably more than you really want to know .....

There are very few of us who know just what all the Czars' do up in D.C.................Here is their names and job descriptions......should be educational to ALL AMERICANS............no matter what your political agenda.......if you resent this list, then get angry at the one who put these characters on the payroll. OBAMA'S "CZARS"-- Read who they are and realize what they want to do.

OBAMA'S CZARS
CZAR, Czar Position, Summary

Richard Holbrook, AfghanistanCzar
Ultra liberal anti gun former Gov. of New Mexico. Pro Abortion and legal drug use. Dissolve the 2nd Amendment

<u>Ed Montgomery</u>, Auto recovery Czar
Black radical anti business activist. Affirmative Action and Job Preference for blacks. Univ of Maryland Business School Dean teaches US business has caused world poverty. ACORN board member. Communist DuBois Club member.

<u>Jeffrey Crowley</u>, AIDS Czar
Radical Homosexual.. A Gay Rights activist. Believes in Gay Marriage and especially, a Special Status for homosexuals only, including complete free health care for gays.

<u>Alan Berlin</u>, Border Czar
The former failed superintendent of San Diego . Ultra Liberal friend of Hilary Clinton. Served as Border Czar under Janet Reno - to keep borders open to illegal's without interference from US

<u>David J. Hayes</u>, California Water Czar
Sr. Fellow of radical environmentalist group, "Progress Policy". No training or experience in water management whatsoever.

Ron Bloom, Car Czar
Auto Union worker. Anti business & anti nuclear. Has worked hard to force US auto makers out of business. Sits on the Board of Chrysler which is now Auto Union owned. How did this happen?

Dennis Ross, Central Region Czar
Believes US policy has caused Mid East wars. Obama apologist to the world. Anti gun and completely pro abortion.

Lynn Rosenthal, Domestic Violence Czar
Director of the National Network to End Domestic Violence. Vicious anti male feminist. Supported male castration. Imagine?

Gil Kerlikowske, Drug Czar
devoted lobbyist for every restrictive gun law proposal, Former Chief of Police in Liberal Seattle. Believes no American should own a firearm. Supports legalization of all drugs

Paul Volcker, EconomicCzar
Head of Fed Reserve under Jimmy Carter when US economy nearly failed. Obama appointed head of the Economic Recovery Advisory Board which engineered the Obama economic disaster to US economy. Member of anti business "Progressive Policy" organization

Carol Browner, Energy and Environment Czar
Political Radical Former head of EPA - known for anti-business activism. Strong anti-gun ownership.

Joshua DuBois, Faith Based Czar
Political Black activist-Degree in Black Nationalism. Anti gun ownership lobbyist.

Cameron Davis, Great LakesCzar
Chicago radical anti business environmentalist. Blames George Bush for "Poisoning the water that minorities have to drink." No experience or training in water management. Former ACORN Board member (what does that tell us?)

<u>Van Jones</u>, Green Jobs Czar
(since resigned).. Black activist Member of American communist Party and San Francisco Communist Party who said Geo Bush caused the 911 attack and wanted Bush investigated by the World Court for war crimes. Black activist with strong anti-white views.

<u>Daniel Fried</u>, Guantanamo Closure Czar Human Rights activist for Foreign Terrorists. Believes America has caused the war on terrorism. Believes terrorists have rights above and beyond Americans.

<u>Nancy-Ann DeParle</u>. Health Czar
Former head of Medicare / Medicaid. Strong Health Care Rationing proponent. She is married to a reporter for The New York Times.

<u>Vivek Kundra</u>, Information Czar
Born in New Delhi, India. Controls all public information, including labels and news releases. Monitors all private Internet emails. (hello?)

Todd Stern, International Climate Czar
Anti business former White House chief of Staff- Strong supportrer of the Kyoto Accord. Pushing hard for Cap and Trade. Blames US business for Global warming. Anti- US business prosperity.

Dennis Blair, Intelligence Czar
Ret Navy. Stopped US guided missile program as "provocative". Chair of ultra liberal "Council on Foreign Relations" which blames American organizations for regional wars.

George Mitchell, Mideast Peace Czar
Fmr. Sen from Maine Left wing radical. Has said Israel should be split up into "2 or 3 " smaller more manageable plots". (God forbid) A true Anti-nuclear anti-gun & pro homosexual "special rights" advocate

Kenneth Feinberg, Pay Czar
Chief of Staff to TED KENNEDY. Lawyer who got rich off the 911 victims payoffs. (horribly true)

<u>Cass Sunstein</u>, Regulatory Czar
Liberal activist judge believes free speech needs to be limited for the "common good". Essentially against 1st amendment. Rules against personal freedoms many times -like private gun ownership and right to free speech.

John Holdren, Science Czar
Fierce ideological environmentalist, Sierra Club, Anti business activist. Claims US business has caused world poverty. No Science training.

<u>Earl Deviancy</u>, Stimulus Accountability Czar
Spent career trying to take guns away from American citizens. Believes in Open Borders to Mexico . Author of statement blaming US gun stores for drug war in Mexico .

<u>J. Scott Gration</u>, Sudan Czar
Native of Democratic Republic of Congo. Believes US does little to help Third World countries. Council of foreign

relations, asking for higher US taxes to support United Nations

Herb Allison, TARP Czar
Fannie May CEO responsible for the US recession by using real estate mortgages to back up the US stock market. Caused millions of people to lose their life savings.

John Brennan, Terrorism Czar
Anti CIA activist.   No training in diplomatic or gov. affairs. Believes Open Borders to Mexico and a dialog with terrorists and has suggested Obama disband US military

Aneesh Chopra, Technology Czar
No Technology training.   Worked for the Advisory Board Company, a health care think tank for hospitals. Anti doctor activist. Supports Obama Health care Rationing and salaried doctors working exclusively for the Gov. health care plan

Adolfo Carrion Jr., Urban Affairs Czar-Puerto Rican born Anti American activist and leftist group member in Latin America . Millionaire "slum lord" of the Bronx , NY. Owns many lavish homes and condos which he got from "sweetheart" deals with labor unions. Wants higher taxes on middle class to pay for minority housing and health care

Ashton Carter, Weapons Czar
Leftist. Wants all private weapons in US destroyed. Supports UN ban on firearms ownership in America .. No Other "policy"

Gary Samore, WMD Policy Czar
Former US Communist. Wants US to destroy all WMD unilaterally as a show of good faith. Has no other "policy".

How lucky are we that these are the people who are helping President Obama in the RUNNING of our country and the White House?

ARE YOU MAD YET?

****

This next article was written by a young student who is able to really hit the nail on the head. Many of us believe that this political fight is between us older folks who have been around and know the score. It is refreshing to find out that young minds can also think along the "common sense" lines.

**

DIVORCE AGREEMENT

THIS IS SO INCREDIBLY WELL PUT AND I CAN HARDLY BELIEVE IT'S BY A YOUNG PERSON, A STUDENT!!!

WHATEVER HE RUNS FOR, I'LL VOTE FOR HIM.

American liberals, leftists, social progressives, socialists, Marxists and Obama supporters, etc.

We have stuck together since the late 1950's, but the whole of this latest election process has made me realize that I want a divorce..... I know we tolerated each other for many years for the sake of future generations, but sadly, this relationship has run its course.

Our two ideological sides of America cannot and will not ever agree on what is right so let's just end it on friendly terms. We can smile and chalk it up to irreconcilable differences and go our own way.

Here is a model separation agreement:

Our two groups can equitably divide up the country by landmass each taking a portion. That will be the difficult part, but I am sure our two sides can come to a friendly agreement. After that, it should be relatively easy! Our respective representatives can effortlessly divide other assets since both sides have such distinct and disparate tastes.

We don't like redistributive taxes so you can keep them. You are welcome to the liberal judges and the ACLU.

Since you hate guns and war, we'll take our firearms, the cops, the NRA and the military.

You can keep Oprah, Michael Moore and Rosie O'Donnell (You are, however, responsible for finding a bio-diesel vehicle big enough to move all three of them).

We'll keep the capitalism, greedy corporations, pharmaceutical companies, Wal-Mart and Wall Street. You can have your beloved homeless, homeboys, hippies and illegal aliens. We'll keep the hot Alaskan hockey moms, greedy CEO's and rednecks.

We'll keep the Bibles and give you NBC and Hollywood

You can make nice with Iran and Palestine and we'll retain the right to invade and hammer places that threaten us...

You can have the peaceniks and war protesters.

When our allies or our way of life are under assault, we'll help provide them security.

We'll keep our Judeo-Christian values... You are welcome to Islam, Scientology, Humanism and Shirley McClaine.

You can also have the U.N.. but we will no longer be paying the bill.

We'll keep the SUVs, pickup trucks and oversized luxury cars. You can take every Subaru station wagon you can find.

You can give everyone healthcare if you can find any practicing doctors. We'll continue to believe health care is a luxury and not a right.

We'll keep The Battle Hymn of the Republic and the National Anthem. I'm sure you'll be happy to substitute â_Imagine_, _I'd Like to Teach_ _the World to_ Sing, _Kum Ba Ya_ or _We Are the World_.â

We'll practice trickle down economics and you can give trickle up poverty your best shot.

Since it so often offends you, we'll keep our history, our name and our flag.

Would you agree to this? If so, please pass it along to other like minded liberal and conservative patriots and if you do not agree, just hit delete. In the spirit of friendly parting, I'll bet you answer which one of us will need whose help in 15 years.

Sincerely,

John J. Wall
Law Student and an American

P.S. Also, please take Ted Turner, Sean Penn, Martin Sheen, Barbara Streisand, & Jane Fonda with you..
P. P. S. And we won't have to press 1 for English.

****

Now let's hear from a 95 year old veteran who also knows what he is talking about.

**

WW II Battleship sailor tells Obama to shape up or ship out !

This venerable and much honored WW II vet is well known in Hawaii for his seventy-plus years of service to patriotic organizations and causes all over the country. A humble man without a political bone in his body, he has never spoken out before about a government official, until now. He dictated this letter to a friend, signed it and mailed it to the president.

Dear President Obama,

My name is Harold Estes, approaching 95 on December 13 of this year. People meeting me for the first time don't believe my age because I remain wrinkle free and pretty much mentally alert.

I enlisted in the U.S. Navy in 1934 and served proudly before, during and after WW II retiring as a Master Chief Bos'n Mate. Now I live in a "rest home" located on the western end of Pearl Harbor , allowing me to keep alive the memories of 23 years of service to my country.

One of the benefits of my age, perhaps the only one, is to speak my mind, blunt and direct even to the head man.

So here goes.

I am amazed, angry and determined not to see my country die before I do, but you seem hell bent not to grant me that wish.

I can't figure out what country you are the president of.

You fly around the world telling our friends and enemies despicable lies like:
" We're no longer a Christian nation"
' America is arrogant" - (Your wife even announced to the world," America is

mean-spirited." Please tell her to try preaching that nonsense to 23 generations of our war dead buried all over the globe who died for no other reason than to free a whole lot of strangers from tyranny and hopelessness.)

I'd say shame on the both of you, but I don't think you like America, nor do I see an ounce of gratefulness in anything you do, for the obvious gifts this country has given you. To be without shame or gratefulness is a dangerous thing for a man sitting in the White House.

After 9/11 you said," America hasn't lived up to her ideals."

Which ones did you mean? Was it the notion of personal liberty that 11,000 farmers and shopkeepers died for to win independence from the British? Or maybe the ideal that no man should be a slave to another man, that 500,000 men died for in the Civil War? I hope you didn't mean the ideal 470,000 fathers, brothers, husbands, and a lot of fellas I knew personally died for in WWII, because we felt real strongly about not letting any nation push us around, because we stand for freedom.

I don't think you mean the ideal that says equality is better than discrimination. You know the one that a whole lot of white people understood when they helped to get you elected.

Take a little advice from a very old geezer, young man.

Shape up and start acting like an American. If you don't, I'll do what I can to see you get shipped out of that fancy rental on Pennsylvania Avenue . You were elected to lead not to bow, apologize and kiss the hands of murderers and corrupt leaders who still treat their people like slaves.

And just who do you think you are telling the American people not to jump to conclusions and condemn that Muslim major who killed 13 of his fellow soldiers and wounded dozens more. You mean you don't want us to do what you did when that white cop used force to subdue that black college professor in Massachusetts , who was putting up a fight? You don't mind offending the police calling them stupid but you don't want us to offend Muslim fanatics by calling them what they are, terrorists.

One more thing. I realize you never served in the military and never had to defend your country with your life, but you're the Commander-in-Chief now, son. Do your job. When your battle-hardened field General asks you for 40,000 more troops to complete the mission, give them to him. But if you're not in this fight to win, then get out. The life of one American soldier is not worth the best political strategy you're thinking of.

You could be our greatest president because you face the greatest challenge ever presented to any president.

You're not going to restore American greatness by bringing back our bloated economy.   That's not our greatest threat. Losing the heart and soul of who we are as Americans is our big fight now.

And I sure as hell don't want to think my president is the enemy in this final battle...

Sincerely,

Harold B. Estes

 Snopes confirms as true:

http://www.snopes.com/politics/soapbox/haroldestes.asp

****

   In the one year plus of BO's administration he has said a great deal and many were inflammatory. Take for instance when he thought the troops should take out their own insurance. After all no one forced them to join the military.

**

THIS HAS GOT TO BE THE MOST OUTRA-GEOUS STATEMENT EVER MADE BY A PUB-LIC OFFICIAL, LET ALONE BY THE PRESI-DENT OF THE UNITED STATES.   AND THIS GUY IS OUR "COMMANDER IN CHIEF".
HERE IS HIS RESPONSE WHEN HE BACKED OFF FROM HIS DECISION TO REQUIRE THE MILITARY PAY FOR THEIR WAR INJURIES.

Bad press, including major mockery of the plan by comedian Jon Stewart, led to President Obama abandoning his proposal to require veterans carry pri-vate health insurance to cover the esti-mated $540 million annual cost to the federal government of treatment for inju-ries to military personnel received during their tours on active duty. The President admitted that he was puzzled by the magnitude of the opposition to his proposal.

"Look, it's an all volunteer force," Obama complained.

"Nobody made these guys go to war.

They had to have known and accepted the risks.
Now they whine about bearing the costs of their choice? It doesn't compute.." "I thought these were people who were proud to sacrifice for their country, "Obama continued. "I wasn't asking for blood, just money. With the country facing the worst financial crisis in its history, I'd have thought that the patriotic thing to do would be to try to help reduce the nation's deficit. I guess I underestimated the selfishness of some of my fellow Americans."

Please pass this on to every vet and their families whom you know.

REMEMBER THIS STATEMENT... "Nobody made these guys go to war. They had to have known and accepted the risks.

Now they whine about bearing the costs of their choice?"

If this jerk thinks he will ever get another vote from anyone who is or has been associated with the military service he's nuts.. If you or a family member is serving or has served their country, please send this to them.

I'm guessing that everyone, other than the 20-25 percent hardcore liberals in the US , will agree that this is another example of why Obama is the worst president in American history. Remind everyone over-and-over how this man thinks, while he bows to the Saudi Arabian king. Obama's Private Insurance Proposal for Military

"The democracy will cease to exist when you take away from those who are willing to work and give to those who would not."
Thomas Jefferson

****

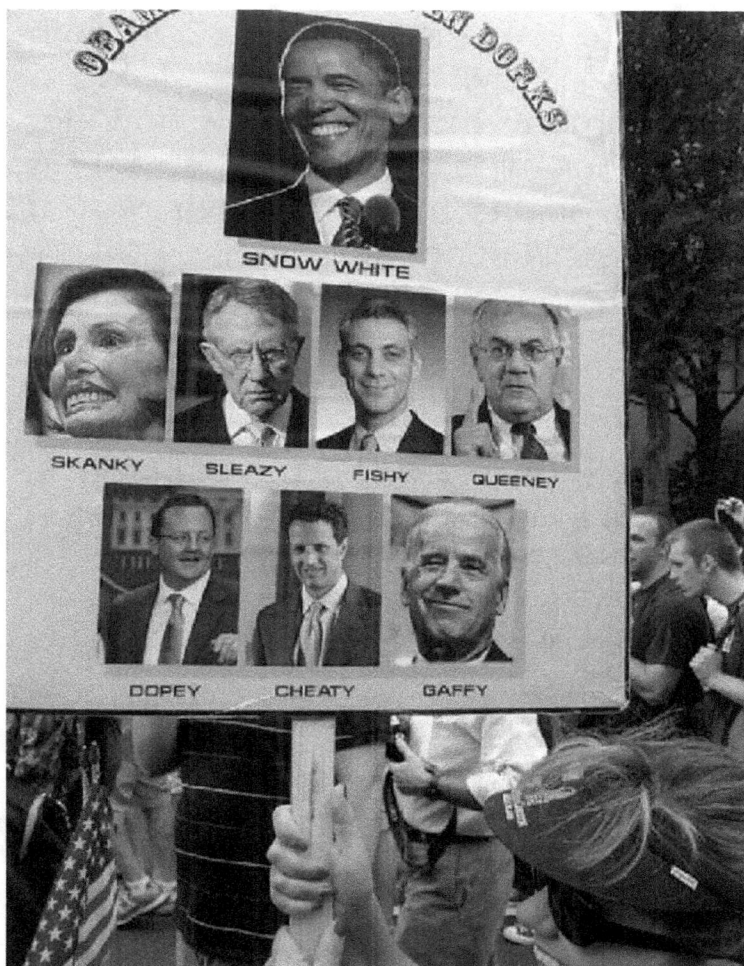

Forgive us Disney...but...The BEST "TEA PARTY" SIGN YET!
Obama and the Seven Dorks

Since Pelosi is glued to BO in both mind and body, "Skanky" has stated a few comments that really show how deformed her mind really is. This really is testimony to the mental deficiency that is prevalent in our government.

**

Pelosi: It's Cheaper to Treat Teens for Drug Use Than Interdict Drugs at Border
Thursday, May 06, 2010
By Edwin Mora

House Speaker Nancy Pelosi (AP Photo/ Manuel Balce Ceneta)
(CNSNews.com) - While pointing out that it is the responsibility of the federal government to secure the U.S.-Mexico border, House Speaker Nancy Pelosi (D.-Calif.) said Thursday it is cheaper to treat teens for drug use than it is to interdict drugs being smuggled across the border.

CNSNews.com pointed out to the speaker at her weekly press briefing that a recent Justice Department report indicated that one in five U.S. teenagers used drugs last year, and then asked: "Are you committed to sealing the border against the influx of illegal drugs from Mexico and, if so, do you have a target date in mind for getting that done?"

"Well if your question is about drugs, I'm for reducing demand in the United States," said Pelosi. "That is what our responsibility is on this subject. The RAND Corporation a few years ago did a report that said it would be much less expensive for us to, through prevention first and foremost, but through treatment on demand to reduce demand in our country, is the cheapest way to solve this problem.

And here is another:

Pelosi to Aspiring Musicians: Quit Your Job, Taxpayers Will Cover Your Health Care
Friday, May 14, 2010
By Nicholas Ballasy, Video Reporter

(CNSNews.com) - House Speaker Nancy Pelosi said this week that thanks to the new health-care reform law, musicians and other creative types could quit their jobs and focus on developing their talents because taxpayers would fund their health care coverage.

"We see it as an entrepreneurial bill," Pelosi said, "a bill that says to someone, if you want to be creative and be a musician or whatever, you can leave your work, focus on your talent, your skill, your passion, your aspirations because you will have health care."

Pelosi made the remarks while speaking at the Capitol on Wednesday to the Asian American and Pacific Islanders Summit.

****

Recently BO gave the order to take down our flag in Haiti so we wouldn't offend anyone. This is not hard to believe since he doesn't respect the flag or those that fight for it. It is also noted that no other country took their flag down.

**

Following the devastating earthquake in Haiti, the United States rushed in to help - with money, medicine, and manpower. To date, we've already given over $179 million in humanitarian aid... but Barack Obama has just ordered all U.S. installations to take down their American flags, lest we be seen as an "occupying army" rather than "international partners."

It is patently appalling that a president of the United States would consider our flag to be a symbol of militaristic takeovers and colonialism, especially when serving (to a greater degree than any other nation on Earth) a humanitarian purpose.

Additionally, who would think we'd want to occupy Haiti?!
No other country giving aid in Haiti has lowered its flag. But then again, no other

country has a leader who is offended by their own flag.

****

Several letters to BO that need passing along.

**

Interesting summary of America today....
"I'm 63 and Im Tired"
by Robert A. Hall

I'm 63. Except for one semester in college when jobs were scarce and a six-month period when I was between jobs, but job-hunting every day, I've worked, hard, since I was 18. Despite some health challenges, I still put in 50-hour weeks, and haven't called in sick in seven or eight years. I make a good salary, but I didn't inherit my job or my income, and I worked to get where I am. Given the economy, there's no retirement in sight, and I'm tired. Very tired.

I'm tired of being told that I have to "spread the wealth" to people who don't have my work ethic. I'm tired of being told the government will take the money I earned, by force if necessary, and give it to people too lazy to earn it.

I'm tired of being told that I have to pay more taxes to "keep people in their homes." Sure, if they lost their jobs or got sick, I'm willing to help. But if they bought McMansions at three times the price of our paid-off, $250,000 condo, on one-third of my salary, then let the left-wing Congress-critters who passed Fannie and Freddie and the Community Reinvestment Act that created the bubble help them with their own money.

I'm tired of being told how bad America is by left-wing millionaires like Michael Moore, George Soros and Hollywood Entertainers who live in luxury because of the opportunities America offers. In thirty years, if they get their way, the United States will have the economy of Zimbabwe , the freedom of the press of

China , the crime and violence of Mexico , the tolerance for Christian people of Iran , and the freedom of speech of Venezuela .

I'm tired of being told that Islam is a "Religion of Peace," when every day I can read dozens of stories of Muslim men killing their sisters, wives and daughters for their family "honor"; of Muslims rioting over some slight offense; of Muslims murdering Christian and Jews because they aren't "believers"; of Muslims burning schools for girls; of Muslims stoning teenage rape victims to death for "adultery"; of Muslims mutilating the genitals of little girls; all in the name of Allah, because the Qur'an and Shari'a law tells them to.

I'm tired of being told that "race doesn't matter" in the post-racial world of Obama, when it's all that matters in affirmative action jobs, lower college admission and graduation standards for minorities (harming them the most), government contract set-asides, tolerance for the ghetto culture of violence and fatherless children that hurts minorities more than anyone, and in the appointment of U.S. Senators from Illinois.

I think it's very cool that we have a black president and that a black child is doing her homework at the desk where Lincoln wrote the Emancipation Proclamation. I just wish the black president was Condi Rice, or someone who believes more in freedom and the individual and less arrogantly of an all-knowing government.

I'm tired of a news media that thinks Bush's fundraising and inaugural expenses were obscene, but that think Obama's, at triple the cost, were wonderful; that thinks Bush exercising daily was a waste of presidential time, but Obama exercising is a great example for the public to control weight and stress; that picked over every line of Bush's military records, but never demanded that Kerry release his; that slammed Palin, with two years as governor, for being too inexperienced for VP, but touted

Obama with three years as senator as potentially the best president ever. Wonder why people are dropping their subscriptions or switching to Fox News? Get a clue. I didn't vote for Bush in 2000, but the media and Kerry drove me to his camp in 2004.

I'm tired of being told that out of "tolerance for other cultures" we must let Saudi Arabia use our oil money to fund mosques and madrassa Islamic schools to preach hate in America , while no American group is allowed to fund a church, synagogue or religious school in Saudi Arabia to teach love and tolerance.

I'm tired of being told I must lower my living standard to fight global warming, which no one is allowed to debate. My wife and I live in a two-bedroom apartment and carpool together five miles to our jobs. We also own a three-bedroom condo where our daughter and granddaughter live. Our carbon footprint is about 5% of Al Gore's, and if you're greener than Gore, you're green enough.

I'm tired of being told that drug addicts have a disease, and I must help support and treat them, and pay for the damage they do. Did a giant germ rush out of a dark alley, grab them, and stuff white powder up their noses while they tried to fight it off? I don't think Gay people choose to be Gay, but I damn sure think druggies chose to take drugs. And I'm tired of harassment from cool people treating me like a freak when I tell them I never tried marijuana.

I'm tired of illegal aliens being called "undocumented workers," especially the ones who aren't working, but are living on welfare or crime. What's next? Calling drug dealers, "Undocumented Pharmacists"? And, no, I'm not against Hispanics. Most of them are Catholic, and it's been a few hundred years since Catholics wanted to kill me for my religion. I'm willing to fast track for citizenship any Hispanic person, who can speak English, doesn't have a criminal record and who is self-supporting without family on welfare, or who serves honorably for three years in our military.... Those are the citizens we need.

I'm tired of latte liberals and journalists, who would never wear the uniform of the Republic themselves, or let their entitlement-handicapped kids near a recruiting station, trashing our military. They and their kids can sit at home, never having to make split-second deci-sions under life and death circum-stances, and bad mouth better people than themselves. Do bad things happen in war? You bet. Do our troops some-times misbehave? Sure. Does this com-pare with the atrocities that were the policy of our enemies for the last fifty years and still are? Not even close. So here's the deal. I'll let myself be sub-jected to all the humiliation and abuse that was heaped on terrorists at Abu Ghraib or Gitmo, and the critics can let themselves be subject to captivity by the Muslims, who tortured and beheaded Daniel Pearl in Pakistan, or the Muslims who tortured and murdered Marine Lt. Col. William Higgins in Lebanon, or the Muslims who ran the blood-spattered Al Qaeda torture rooms our troops found in Iraq, or the Muslims who cut off the heads of schoolgirls in Indonesia, because the girls were Christian. Then we'll compare notes. British and American soldiers are the only troops in history that civilians came to for help and handouts, instead of hiding from in fear.

I'm tired of people telling me that their party has a corner on virtue and the other party has a corner on corruption. Read the papers; bums are bipartisan. And I'm tired of people telling me we need bipartisanship. I live in Illinois , where the "Illinois Combine" of Democrats has worked to loot the public for years. Not to mention the tax cheats in Obama's cabinet.

I'm tired of hearing wealthy athletes, entertainers and politicians of both parties talking about innocent mistakes, stupid mistakes or youthful mistakes, when we all know they think their only mistake was getting caught. I'm tired of people with a sense of entitlement, rich or poor.

Speaking of poor, I'm tired of hearing people with air-conditioned homes, color TVs and two cars called poor. The majority of Americans didn't have that in 1970, but we didn't know we were "poor." The poverty pimps have to keep changing the definition of poor to keep the dollars flowing.

I'm real tired of people who don't take responsibility for their lives and actions. I'm tired of hearing them blame the government, or discrimination or big-whatever for their problems.

Yes, I'm damn tired. But I'm also glad to be 63. Because, mostly, I'm not going to have to see the world these people are making. I'm just sorry for my granddaughter.

Robert A. Hall is a Marine Vietnam veteran who served five terms in the Massachusetts State Senate.

****

I can't possibly not include this next letter. In fact there are several you need to read:

**

A retired Constitutional lawyer has read the entire proposed healthcare bill. Read his conclusions. This is stunning!

The Truth About the Health Care Bills - Michael Connelly, Ret. Constitutional Attorney

Well, I have done it! I have read the entire text of proposed House Bill 3200: The Affordable Health Care Choices Act of

2009. I studied it with particular emphasis from my area of expertise, constitutional law. I was frankly concerned that parts of the proposed law that were being discussed might be unconstitutional. What I found was far worse than what I had heard or expected.

To begin with, much of what has been said about the law and its implications is in fact true, despite what the Democrats and the media are saying. The law does provide for rationing of health care, particularly where senior citizens and other classes of citizens are involved, free health care for illegal immigrants, free abortion services, and probably forced participation in abortions by members of the medical profession.

The Bill will also eventually force private insurance companies out of business, and put everyone into a government run system.
All decisions about personal health care will ultimately be made by federal bureaucrats, and most of them will not be

health care professionals.   Hospital admissions, payments to physicians, and allocations of necessary medical devices will be strictly controlled by the government.

However, as scary as all of that is, it just scratches the surface.   In fact, I have concluded that this legislation really has no intention of providing affordable health care choices. Instead it is a convenient cover for the most massive transfer of power to the Executive Branch of government that has ever occurred, or even been contemplated If this law or a similar one is adopted, major portions of the Constitution of the United States will effectively have been destroyed.

The first thing to go will be the masterfully crafted balance of power between the Executive, Legislative, and Judicial branches of the U.S. Government.. The Congress will be transferring to the Obama Administration authority in a number of different areas over the lives of the American people, and the businesses they own.

The irony is that the Congress doesn't have any authority to legislate in most of those areas to begin with! I defy anyone to read the text of the U.S. Constitution and find any authority granted to the members of Congress to regulate health care.

This legislation also provides for access, by the appointees of the Obama administration, of all of your personal healthcare direct violation of the specific provisions of the 4th Amendment to the Constitution information, your personal financial information, and the information of your employer, physician, and hospital.   All of this is protecting against unreasonable searches and seizures. You can also forget about the right to privacy. That will have been legislated into oblivion regardless of what the 3rd and 4th Amendments may provide...

If you decide not to have healthcare insurance, or if you have private insurance that is not deemed acceptable to the Health Choices Administrator appointed by Obama, there will be a tax imposed on you. It is called a tax instead of a fine because of the intent to avoid application of the due process clause of the 5th Amendment. However, that doesn't work because since there is nothing in the law that allows you to contest or appeal the imposition of the tax, it is definitely depriving someone of property without the due process of law.

So, there are three of those pesky amendments that the far left hate so much, out the original ten in the Bill of Rights, that are effectively nullified by this law It doesn't stop there though.

The 9th Amendment that provides: The enumeration in the Constitution, of certain rights, shall not be construed to deny or disparage others retained by the people;
The 10th Amendment states: The powers not delegated to the United States by

the Constitution, nor prohibited by it to the States, are preserved to the States respectively, or to the people. Under the provisions of this piece of Congressional handiwork neither the people nor the states are going to have any rights or powers at all in many areas that once were theirs to control.

I could write many more pages about this legislation, but Ithink you get the idea. This is not about health care; it is about seizing power and limiting rights...

Article 6 of the Constitution requires the members of both houses of Congress to "be bound by oath or affirmation to support the Constitution." If I was a member of Congress I would not be able to vote for this legislation or anything like it, without feeling I was violating that sacred oath or affirmation. If I voted for it anyway, I would hope the American people would hold me accountable.

For those who might doubt the nature of this threat, I suggest they consult the source, the US Constitution, and Bill of Rights. There you can see exactly what we are about to have taken from us.

Michael Connelly
Retired attorney,
Constitutional Law Instructor
Carrollton , Texas

****

**

Who would have thought, and yet many are thinking it.

By Lou Pritchett,   Procter & Gamble

A LETTER FROM A PROCTER   AND GAM-
BLE EXECUTIVE TO THE PRESIDENT*

THE LAST SENTENCE IS THE   MOST CHILL-
ING

Lou Pritchett is one of corporate Amer-
ica 's true living legends- an acclaimed author, dynamic teacher and one of the

world's highest rated speakers. Successful corporate executives   everywhere recognize him as the foremost leader in change management..   Lou changed the way America does business by creating an audacious concept that came to be known as "partnering." Pritchett rose from soap   salesman to Vice-President, Sales and Customer Development for   Procter and Gamble and over the course of 36 years, made   corporate history.

AN OPEN LETTER TO
PRESIDENT OBAMA

Dear President Obama:

You are the thirteenth President under whom I have lived and unlike
any of the others, you truly scare me.

You scare me because after months of exposure, I know nothing about you.

You scare me because I do not know how you paid for   your expensive Ivy

League education and your upscale life-style and housing with no visible signs of support.

You scare me because you did not spend the formative   years of youth growing up in America and culturally you are not an American.

You scare me because you have never run a company or met a payroll.

You scare me because you have never had military experience, thus don't understand it at its core.

You scare me because you lack humility and 'class', always blaming others.

You scare me because for over half your life you have aligned yourself with radical extremists who hate America   and you refuse to publicly denounce these radicals who wish to see America fail..

You scare me because you are a cheer-leader for the   'blame America ' crowd and deliver this message abroad.

You scare me because you want to change America to a European style country where the government sector dominates instead of the private sector.

You scare me because you want to replace our health care system with a government controlled one.

You scare me because you prefer 'wind mills' to responsibly capitalizing on our own vast oil, coal and shale reserves.

You scare me because you want to kill the American capitalist goose that lays the golden egg which provides the highest standard of living in the world.

You scare me because you have begun to use 'extortion' tactics against certain banks and corporations.

You scare me because your own political party shrinks from challenging you on your wild and irresponsible spending proposals.

You scare me because you will not openly listen to or even consider opposing points of view from intelligent people.

You scare me because you falsely believe that you are both omnipotent and omniscient.

You scare me because the media gives you a free pass on everything you do.

You scare me because you demonize and want to silence the Limbaugh's, Hannitys, O'Reillys and Becks who offer opposing, conservative points of view.

You scare me because you prefer controlling over governing.

Finally, you scare me because if you serve a second term I will probably not feel safe in writing a similar letter in a few more years.

Lou Pritchett
*

*

This letter was sent to the NY Times but they never acknowledged it
Big   surprise. Since it hit the internet, however, it has had over
500,000 hits. All that is necessary for evil to succeed is that good men do nothing
It's happening right   now.*
http://www.snopes.com/politics/soapbo x / y o u s c a r e m e . a s p
<http://www.snopes.com/politics/soapb ox/youscareme.asp>

****

In order to understand the depth of moronic goings-on in Washington under BO's leadership, the following takes the cake:

**

In 1952, President Truman established one day a year as a National Day of Prayer.

In 1988, President Reagan designated the first Thursday in May of each year as the National Day of Prayer.

In June 2007, (then) Presidential candidate Barack Obama declared that the USA was no longer a Christian nation.

This year President Obama, canceled the 21st annual National Day of Prayer ceremony at the White House under the ruse of "not wanting to offend anyone".

On September 25, 2009 from 4 am until 7 PM, a National Day of Prayer for the Muslim religion was held on Capitol Hill, beside the White House. There were over 50,000 Muslims that day in DC.

I guess it doesn't matter if "Christians" are offended by this event - we obviously don't count as "anyone" anymore.

The direction this country is headed should strike fear in the heart of every Christian. Especially knowing that the Muslim religion believes that if Christians cannot be converted they should be annihilated.

****

I thought I would throw in something that, I'm sure, all of us agree on. This is something that we all think about, but are afraid to talk about. What would happen if one day - - -

**

WOULDN'T IT BE GREAT TO TURN ON THE TV AND HEAR ANY U.S. PRESIDENT, DEMOCRAT OR REPUBLICAN GIVE THE FOLLOWING SPEECH?

"My Fellow Americans: As you all know, the defeat of the Iraq regime has been completed.

Since congress does not want to spend any more money on this war, our mission in Iraq is complete.

This morning I gave the order for a complete removal of all American forces from Iraq This action will be complete within 30 days. It is now time to begin the reckoning.

Before me, I have two lists. One list contains the names of countries which have stood by our side during the Iraq conflict. This list is short . The United Kingdom , Spain , Bulgaria , Australia , and Poland are some of the countries listed there.

The other list contains every one not on the first list. Most of the world's nations are on that list.. My press secretary will be distributing copies of both lists later this evening.

Let me start by saying that effective immediately, foreign aid to those nations on List 2 ceases immediately and indefinitely. The money saved during the first year alone will pretty much pay for the costs of the Iraqi war. THEN EVERY YEAR THERE AFTER IT'll GO TO OUR SOCIAL SECURITY SYSTEM SO IT WONT GO BROKE IN 20 YEARS.

The American people are no longer going to pour money into third world Hell holes and watch those government leaders grow fat on corruption.

Ron Berger   241

Need help with a famine ? Wrestling with an epidemic? Call France .

In the future, together with Congress, I will work to redirect this money toward solving the vexing social problems we still have at home . On that note, a word to terrorist organizations. Screw with us and we will hunt you down and eliminate you and all your friends from the face of the earth..

Thirsting for a gutsy country to terrorize? Try France or maybe China .

I am ordering the immediate severing of diplomatic relations with France , Germany , and Russia .. Thanks for all your help, comrades. We are retiring from NATO as well. Bonne chance, mezamies.

I have instructed the Mayor of New York City to begin towing the many UN diplomatic vehicles located in Manhattan with more than two unpaid parking tickets to sites where those vehicles will be stripped, shredded and crushed. I don't care about whatever treaty pertains to this You creeps have tens of thousands of unpaid tickets. Pay those tickets tomorrow or watch your precious Benzes, Beamers and limos be turned over to some of the finest chop shops in the world. I love New York

A special note to our neighbors. Canada is on List 2. Since we are likely to be seeing a lot more of each other, you folks might want to try not pissing us off for a change.

Mexico is also on List 2 its president and his entire corrupt government really need an attitude adjustment. I will have a couple extra thousand tanks and infantry divisions sitting around Guess where I am going to put 'em? Yep, border security.

Oh, by the way, the United States is abrogating the NAFTA treaty - starting now.

We are tired of the one-way highway. Immediately, we'll be drilling for oil in

Alaska- which will take care of this country's oil needs for decades to come. If you're an environmentalist who opposes this decision, I refer you to List 2 above: pick a country and move there.

It is time for America to focus on its own welfare and its own citizens. Some will accuse us of isolationism. I answer them by saying, 'darn tootin.'

Nearly a century of trying to help folks live a decent life around the world has only earned us the undying enmity of just about everyone on the planet. It is time to eliminate hunger in America It is time to eliminate homelessness in America . To the nations on List 1, a final thought. Thank you guys. We owe you and we won't forget.

To the nations on List 2, a final thought: You might want to learn to speak Arabic.

God bless America .. Thank you and good night."

If you can read this, thank a teacher. If you are reading it in English, thank a soldier.

****

The following is a great synopsis of Sarah Palin. I can only hope that she decides to run for President in 2012. She and Condoleezza Rice would make a great team - don't you think?

**

By Dewie Whetsell, Alaskan Fisherman.
As posted in comments on Greta's article referencing the MOVEON ad about Sarah Palin.

The last 45 of my 66 years I've spent in a commercial fishing town in Alaska . I understand Alaska politics but never understood national politics well until this last year. Here's the breaking point: Neither side of the Palin controversy gets it. It's not about persona, style, rhetoric, it's about doing things. Even Palin supporters never mention the things that I'm about to mention here.

1. Democrats forget when Palin was the Darling of the Democrats, because as soon as Palin took the Governor's office away from a fellow Republican and tough SOB, Frank Murkowski, she tore into the Republican's "Corrupt Bastards Club" (CBC) and sent them packing. Many of them are now residing in State housing and wearing orange jump suits The Democrats reacted by skipping around the yard, throwing confetti and singing, "la la la la" (well, you know how they are). Name another governor in this country that has ever done anything similar.

2. Now with the CBC gone, there were fewer Alaskan politicians to protect the huge, giant oil companies here. So she constructed and enacted a new system of splitting the oil profits called "ACES." Exxon (the biggest corporation in the world) protested and Sarah told them,

"don't let the door hit you in the stern on your way out." They stayed, and Alaska residents went from being merely wealthy to being filthy rich. Of course, the other huge international oil companies meekly fell in line. Again, give me the name of any other governor in the country that has done anything similar.

3. The other thing she did when she walked into the governor's office is she got the list of State requests for federal funding for projects, known as "pork." She went through the list, took 85% of them and placed them in the "when-hell-freezes-over" stack. She let locals know that if we need something built, we'll pay for it ourselves. Maybe she figured she could use the money she got from selling the previous governor's jet because it was extravagant.

Maybe she could use the money she saved by dismissing the governor's cook (remarking that she could cook for her own family), giving back the State vehicle issued to her, maintaining that she already had a car, and dismissing her State provided security force (never mentioning - I imagine - that she's packing heat herself). I'm still waiting to hear the names of those other governors.

4. Now, even with her much-ridiculed "gosh and golly" mannerism, she also managed to put together a totally new approach to getting a natural gas pipeline built which will be the biggest private construction project in the history of North America. No one else could do it although they tried.. If that doesn't impress you, then you're trying too hard to be unimpressed while watching her do things like this while baking up a batch of brownies with her other hand.

5. For 30 years, Exxon held a lease to do exploratory drilling at a place called Point Thompson. They made excuses the entire time why they couldn't start drilling. In truth they were holding it like an investment. No governor for 30 years could make them get started. Then, she told them she was revoking their lease

and kicking them out. They protested and threatened court action. She shrugged and reminded them that she knew the way to the court house. Alaska won again.

6. President Obama wants the nation to be on 25% renewable resources for electricity by 2025. Sarah went to the legislature and submitted her plan for Alaska to be at 50% renewables by 2025. We are already at 25%. I can give you more specifics about things done, as opposed to style and persona Everybody wants to be cool, sound cool, look cool. But that's just a cover-up. I'm still waiting to hear from liberals the names of other governors who can match what mine has done in two and a half years.. I won't be holding my breath.

By the way, she was content to return to AK after the national election and go to work, but the haters wouldn't let her. Now these adolescent screechers are obviously not scuba divers. And no one ever told them what happens when you continually jab and pester a barracuda. Without warning, it will spin around and tear your face off. Shoulda known better.

You have just read the truth about Sarah Palin that sends the media, along with the democrat party, into a wild uncontrolled frenzy to discredit her. I guess they are only interested in skirt chasers, dishonesty, immoral people, liars, womanizers, murderers, and bitter ex-presidents' wives.

So "You go, Girl." I only wish the men in Washington had your guts, determination, honesty, and morals. I rest my case. Only FOOLS listen to the biased media.

****

What's missing in BO's picture compared to the previous four presidents?

That's right...no American flag!!! And I don't believe it was just an accident! It is intentional. So I ask, why is it intentional? He told you he would change America, didn't he?
Vote in November like your future way of life depends on it !

Because It Probably Does!!!!!!!

Time for STILL MORE TEA

Ron Berger   254

Dear America,
I quit.

The New American Dream.

What a dream that would be!

THE GRAND OLD FLAG

I wonder what our flag would do
If it could talk today?
What are the stories from its past?
What would this grand flag say?

"I am held on many poles
Waving proudly in the sky.
I hold my head up straight and tall
As people pass me by".

"I have gone to many wars
I am honored as I can be
When a soldier gives his life
He is proudly wrapped in me".

I am called "Old Glory"
Respected and admired
I wonder why our government
Then feels me undesired

One day they put me on a pole
In a U.S. town
Then set my stars and stripes on fire
While I burned upside down.

Ron Berger   256

Just the other day I found
Flags of other nations
Waving high above me
With greatest expectations

Obama does not wear me
On his presidential suit
Nor does he even care a bit
To honor and salute.

He scorns my very colors
Embarrassed with chagrin
When my name is mentioned
It just seems I cannot win.

But to my fellow citizens
I am still held high
And on this next Memorial Day
Salute as I pass by.

Barbara Cook

Thanks, Barbara

Ron Berger   257

MAY GOD BLESS OUR COUNTRY AND ITS CITIZENS

www.ingramcontent.com/pod-product-compliance
Lightning Source LLC
Chambersburg PA
CBHW060840280326
41934CB00007B/857